LORENZACCIO

*Alfred de Musset
translated and
adapted by
John Strand*

BROADWAY PLAY PUBLISHING INC
New York
www.broadwayplaypublishing.com
info@broadwayplaypublishing.com

LORENZACCIO
© Copyright 2006 John Strand

Cover photo by Richard Termine
First printing: February 2007
I S B N: 978-0-88145-327-0
Book design: Marie Donovan
Word processing: Microsoft Word
Typographic controls: Ventura Publisher
Typeface: Palatino

This version of LORENZACCIO was the world premiere at The Shakespeare Theater, Washington, DC (Michael Kahn, Artistic Director; Nicholas T Goldsborough, Managing Director) on 24 January 2005. The cast and creative contributors were:

LORENZACCIO .... Jeffrey Carlson
DUKE OF FLORENCE .... Robert Cuccioli
SALVIATI .... Bernard Sheredy
MAFEO .... Tyler Pierce
GABRIELLA .... Kim Stauffer
PAOLO .... David Sabin
SOFIA .... Kate Kiley
LOUISA STROZZI .... Colleen Delany
COUNTESS CIBO .... Chandler Vinton
COUNT CIBO .... Ralph Cosham
CARDINAL CIBO .... Michael Rudko
AGNOLO .... Sebastian Rodriguez
VALORI .... Floyd King
CATHERINE DE MEDICI .... Marni Penning
MARIE DE MEDICI .... Tana Hicken
PHILIP STROZZI .... Ted van Griethuysen
PIERO STROZZI .... Pedro Pascal
TEBALDEO .... Aubrey Deeker
BINDO .... J Fred Shiffman
VENTURI .... John Livingston Rolle
SCORON .... David B Heuvelman
NICOLINI .... Bernard Sheredy
RUCCELLI .... Ralph Cosham
COSIMO DE MEDICI .... Sean Brennan

SERVANTS, CITIZENS, *and* CONSPIRATORS *played by the*
ensemble.

Director . . . . Michael Kahn
Sets design . . . . Ming Cho Lee
Costumes . . . . Murrell Horton
Lighting . . . . Howell Binkley
Sound . . . . Scott Killian

I am grateful to Michael Kahn for lending to this project
the impressive resources of The Shakespeare Theater
and assembling so talented a cast and design team.
But I am especially grateful for his expert knowledge of
how to make the classical text live and breathe on stage.
In this he is second to none.
J S

CHARACTERS

in order of appearance

LORENZO DE MEDICI, *known as* LORENZACCIO
ALESSANDRO DE MEDICI, DUKE *of Florence*
SALVIATI, *member of the* DUKE'*s entourage*
GABRIELLA, *a virgin*
MAFEO, *a citizen of Florence*
PAOLO, *a cloth seller*
SOFIA, *his wife*
LOUISA STROZZI, *daughter to* PHILIP
COUNTESS CIBO
COUNT CIBO
CARDINAL CIBO, *brother to the* COUNT
AGNOLO, *a messenger*
VALORI, *papal envoy*
CATHERINE DE MEDICI, *sister to* LORENZO
MARIE DE MEDICI, LORENZO'*s mother*
PHILIP STROZZI, *patriarch of Florentine nobility*
PIERO STROZZI, *son to* PHILIP
TEBALDEO, *a painter*
BINDO, *citizen of Florence*
VENTURI, *a merchant*
CONSPIRATOR 1
CONSPIRATOR 2
CONSPIRATOR 3
SCORON, *servant to* LORENZO
NICOLINI, *a royal counselor*
RUCCELLI, *a royal counselor*
COSIMO DE MEDICI, *new Duke of Florence*

With doubling, the play can be performed with as few as 12 actors: 8 men and 4 women. They play a total of 27 roles.

Suggested Doubling:

Actor 1	LORENZO
2	ALESSANDRO, DUKE OF FLORENCE
3	SALVIATI/BINDO/CONSPIRATOR 1/NICOLINI
4	MAFEO/AGNOLO/TEBALDEO/VENTURI/COSIMO
5	PAOLO/VALORI/CONSPIRATOR 2
6	CARDINAL CIBO/CONSPIRATOR 3
7	COUNT CIBO/PHILIP STROZZI/RUCCELLI
8	PIERO STROZZI/SCORON
Actress 1	GABRIELLA/CATHERINE
2	SOFIA/MARIE
3	LOUISA STROZZI
4	COUNTESS CIBO

SETTING

The play takes place in Florence and Venice in 1537

TRANSLATOR'S NOTE

Alfred de Musset was born in Paris in 1810 and died there in 1857. The period of his best writing, much like his life, was brief and marked by passion, intensity and a tendency toward self-destruction. From 1833 to 1837 he produced the poems, plays and the autobiographical novel that secure his place today in the crowded pantheon of great 19th-century French writers. Nothing that he wrote before or after was of equal value.

Musset had a tempestuous relationship with the theater. At the age of eighteen, his poetry and youthful promise had earned him a coveted seat in the *cénacle*, the literary circle that included Victor Hugo. Alfred the young romantic had a high opinion of his own literary ability, and when his first play *La Nuit Vénitienne* was hooted off the stage, he vowed never to write for the theater again, leaving it to struggle along without him, which it managed to do.

Musset's diva act was only half serious. He continued to write plays for publication but not for performance, calling his dramas "Armchair Theater". He wrote them as a deliberate protest against the rigid theatrical conventions of his day. Erring consistently on the side of writerly self-indulgence, the young wounded ego quickly made his point, if not his mark. It would be seventeen years before his plays got on stage in Paris. He obediently rewrote them for the occasion, adding convention where requested. The exception was

LORENZACCIO, written in 1833 and never staged in his lifetime.

Whatever else can be said of Musset's theatrical presumptions, he showed good taste in being a professed admirer of Shakespeare and Schiller. His LORENZACCIO, often referred to as "the French Hamlet," was his homage to Elizabethan theater, as well as a semi-confessional treatise on youthful despair in France under the reign of Louis-Philippe. But aside from such footnotes, LORENZACCIO is a bold, sprawling, magnificent piece of theater. It is unlike anything else written by a French dramatist of the time. Despite its flaws (and they are numerous), at the center of the play is a gripping story of a complex, heroic character bent on political assassination. It is without question the finest thing Musset produced for the stage.

Although the play has been a staple of the European repertoire for more than a century after it was first produced by Sarah Bernhardt in 1896 (heavily adapted, with herself in the title role, to out-diva Musset), LORENZACCIO is virtually unknown to American audiences. This is to our distinct disadvantage.

In the interests of full disclosure, my translation/ adaptation is at least as much adapted as translated. Literal renderings of Musset's original are available in English for anyone wishing to satisfy his curiosity on the topic. These versions are rarely performed, and for good reason. Sitting in an armchair, the reader might accept being led by the nose toward long discussions of the author's social, political, and emotional viewpoints. Sitting in a theater, this is harder to countenance.

I admit, then, to license. But I insist that I have been faithful to the spirit of the play and, I believe, the playwright. The present version, in prose as is the original, is written first to be performed. You have to get out of your armchair if you wish to engage one of the great plays of European theater.

John Strand, Washington, DC, January 2005

for Amanda

1.1

(Night. A walled garden in Florence. Three men are present: the DUKE, SALVIATI, *and* LORENZO. *Each carries a mask worn by guests at a ball.)*

DUKE: Where is she? I have been standing here in the freezing cold for a quarter of an hour. Is she coming or not?

LORENZO: Relax, your highness.

DUKE: You arranged this. Her mother was supposed to send her out at midnight.

LORENZO: If the girl doesn't come, say that I am an ass and her mother is an honorable woman.

DUKE: I paid her a thousand ducats and I was promised a virgin. There's no honesty left in this city.

SALVIATI: Patience, your excellency.

DUKE: I am not going to waste the whole night in some little prostitute's garden. I have to return to the ball, I am the guest of honor.

(He and SALVIATI *turn to go, but* LORENZO's *line stops him.)*

LORENZO: What a treasure, your highness. A child of fifteen. Practically plucked off her mother's tit and delivered up to you for the sole purpose of your pleasure. Only the connoisseur can savor the beauty of it: A naughty little kitten who wants her candy but is afraid to dirty her paws. The thinnest veneer of propriety, like a sheet of ice that cracks at every step—and underneath, a magnificent, raging river.

DUKE: Maybe I'll wait a few minutes more.

SALVIATI: *(To* LORENZO*)* Go try the door. The bitch has been paid for, has she not?

DUKE: Well said, Salviati. Go on, Lorenzo.

*(*LORENZO *exits.)*

MAFEO: *(Off, calling)* Gabriella?

SALVIATI: Someone's coming.

DUKE: Withdraw.

*(*DUKE *puts on mask. They withdraw. Enter* MAFEO, *a citizen.)*

MAFEO: Gabriella?... It was a dream, but so real, it jolted me out of bed. My little sister, in danger, running through the garden in the dark. She wore a necklace of pearls....

(He hears something nearby in the dark.)

MAFEO: Who is there? Show yourself!

*(*SALVIATI *steps from the shadow, followed by the* DUKE*.)*

SALVIATI: This would be the big brother, I assume.

MAFEO: Who are you? What do you want here?

(The girl, in night clothes, wearing a necklace of pearls, runs on, pursued by LORENZO*.)*

GABRIELLA: Mafeo!

MAFEO: Gabriella! Where are you going?!

*(*MAFEO *runs for her, but* SALVIATI *pushes him to the ground as* LORENZO *carries her off.)*

SALVIATI: The little bird has been plucked from the nest.

MAFEO: *(Going for them)* Thieves and rapists!

SALVIATI *(Drawing a knife)* Not so fast, big brother.

MAFEO: You'll hang for this crime, both of you! If there is law still in Florence, I will be avenged! I'll go to the Duke himself!

SALVIATI: The Duke, you say?

MAFEO: I'll tell him the truth about his city—that it's overrun with bandits and assassins—that the daughters of the best families are pulled from their beds at night by bastards like you!

SALVIATI: Shall I stab him, your highness?

DUKE: *(Removes his mask)* No, why trouble the evening with a corpse? Toss the man some coin and send him back to bed. *(He exits.)*

MAFEO: That was the Duke.

SALVIATI: Alessandro de Medici himself. If you want to keep your ears attached to your head, big brother, this meeting never took place.

(SALVIATI gives MAFEO a bag of coins. They exit separately.)

1.2

(Dawn, the next morning. Enter a cloth merchant, PAOLO, and his wife, SOFIA. He pushes a cart. During the following, they hang their wares for the morning market. Offstage, music, laughter, sounds of the masked ball still in progress.

SOFIA: There's a breeze this morning, Paolo, to show off our silks.

PAOLO: Almost dawn and they're still dancing. You hear that? Damn their damnable masked ball, I didn't sleep a wink last night.

SOFIA: The Duke is attending, they say.

PAOLO: Oh, the Duke. The magnificent ruler of Florence is capable of drinking and shouting all night like a college student, that's encouraging. Oh, I feel a hell of a lot better now. Never mind that the people's rights have been stolen and the republic trampled into the mud. We'll just give a masked ball.

SOFIA: *(Looking off stage)* Look. Some of the guests are leaving.

PAOLO: So soon?

SOFIA: Such beautiful costumes.

PAOLO: They'd look a lot better with a silk accessory or two.

SOFIA: That boy there—it's young Palla Ruccelli. And the one next to him—Giorgio Martelli.

PAOLO: Don't gawk, woman, it's cheap.

SOFIA: Oh, there's Piero Strozzi.

PAOLO: *(Gawking)* Where is Piero?

SOFIA: There, look.

PAOLO: That's Piero? He's grown so big.

SOFIA: God keep his father.

PAOLO: Old Philip Strozzi, the last honest man in Florence.

SOFIA: There were so many once.

PAOLO: Before they were banished by the bastard Duke.

SOFIA: Paolo! Be careful, someone will hear you.

PAOLO: Am I not a Florentine? Then I will speak my mind.

SOFIA: Couldn't you whisper your mind?

PAOLO: Florentines will never whisper! A few years ago, this city was like that palace there, proud and well built.

SOFIA: Are you going to use the architecture metaphor again?

PAOLO: All the noble families like the Strozzis were the columns that held it up—

SOFIA: He's using the architecture metaphor again...

PAOLO: —Equal in size, not one taller than the next. Citizens like us could walk in its shadow and not fear the whole thing would collapse on our heads. Then the two worst architects in Europe got their hands on it— the Pope and the Emperor Charles V, God send a plague on them both.

SOFIA: Paolo. People are staring.

PAOLO: They took one of the columns and made a great ugly tower of it—the Medicis. Then they took the bastard Alessandro—

SOFIA: Paolo! Please!

PAOLO: —not even a whole Medici, half Medici and half butcher, and they stuck him in the tower, and made him tyrant of Florence. Now he steals our money, he drinks our wine, he sleeps with our daughters, and he calls in German soldiers—Germans, for God's sake! —To keep him in power and keep a knife to our throats!

SOFIA: Are you through now? We'll just wait here quietly to be arrested. Which direction do you think the soldiers will come from?

PAOLO: Let them banish me. Life in Rome could be no worse than here.

SOFIA: Paolo. They banish the rich. Cloth merchants they skewer on halberds like a baked potato.

PAOLO: Yet am I not a Florentine? Send the biggest, ugliest Germans in Italy, and I'll show them what the merchants of Florence are made of!

(Enter suddenly a young woman, LOUISA STROZZI. She is frantic. She wears a rich gown. She carries a mask, and has come from the ball.)

LOUISA: You there!

PAOLO: *(Bowing, alarmed)* Spare me. I've always loved the Pope!

LOUISA: Hide me! Please!

(Enter SALVIATI.)

SALVIATI: Louisa! Why do you run from me?

LOUISA: I didn't run, Lord Salviati. I came to look at these fine silks.

SALVIATI: Not one of them is fine enough to lay upon your naked flesh.

PAOLO: Actually, my lord, some of these are quite excellent—

SALVIATI: Shut up.

LOUISA: You dishonor me, my lord, with such shameless words.

SALVIATI: What would it take, Louisa, to let me be your chambermaid tonight, and drape your body head to toe in the finest silk?

PAOLO: We're having a special today on Arabian off-white.

SALVIATI: Out of my way.

LOUISA: *(She tries to leave)* I have to return home.

SALVIATI: *(He wraps a piece of silk around her, restraining her)* Not until you tell me when we will sleep together.

LOUISA: Let me go, I warn you.

SOFIA: Let go of her!

SALVIATI: What?

PAOLO: What?

(Enter LORENZO, *dressed as a nun, carrying a bottle.)*

SOFIA: Tell him, Paolo.

PAOLO: Me?

SOFIA: Tell him!

PAOLO: Yes. Uh. My lord, you are discouraging customers. Sir.

*(*SALVIATI *begins to caress her.* LORENZO, *still disguised, throws his bottle at* SALVIATI's *feet.* SALVIATI *turns in anger and* LOUISA *moves away.)*

SALVIATI: Who threw that!? Damn you, you whore!

PAOLO: Sir! That is no way to talk to a holy nun!

*(*LORENZO *pulls off his habit and reveals himself.* LOUISA *gives him a grateful look, and exits.)*

LORENZO: *(Picking up bottle and silk)* Why Salviati. Shopping for presents so early in the morning?

SALVIATI: You and your drunken schoolboy pranks.

LORENZO: Was that Louisa Strozzi you were charming? You seem to have made her angry.

SALVIATI: The day you lose the Duke's favor, Lorenzaccio—that's the day I carve out your cowardly guts.

*(*SALVIATI *pushes roughly past* LORENZO *and exits.)*

LORENZO: He seems a hot-tempered sort, would you not say?

SOFIA: *(Obediently)* Yes, my lord.

PAOLO: *(Obediently)* Yes, my lord.

LORENZO: I hope that his words to the young woman will not be generally known.

SOFIA: No, my lord.

PAOLO: No, my lord.

LORENZO: And so I must ask you, good citizens...

PAOLO: Yes, Lord Lorenzo?

LORENZO: *(Holding up scarf)* Do you have anything in a light blue?

1.3

(Enter COUNT CIBO, *followed by the* COUNTESS *and his brother,* CARDINAL CIBO.)

COUNTESS: Must you go, my darling? Can't you delay your trip?

COUNT: Now is the time to see to the planting. Another season of failed crops will ruin us. I shall soon be back in your arms, Ricarda. Why these tears?

(They embrace.)

CARDINAL: Such dramatics, Countess. You would think your husband were departing for Palestine.

COUNT: Don't mock these beautiful tears, my brother.

CARDINAL: I only wonder at their authenticity. Tears of love?

COUNTESS: Must tears always come from guilt, Cardinal Cibo, or from fear?

COUNT: The best tears come from love. I shall let mine dry during the journey. The vineyards and forests of our old estate may shed tears of their own, Ricarda, when they see you are not with me. *(He starts to leave.)*

COUNTESS: *(Running to him)* Oh, take me with you!

COUNT: An old soldier such as I knows better. The road from the city is not as safe as it once was.

COUNTESS: Don't leave me, Marcelo.

COUNT: *(Concerned at her pleading)* Why, Ricarda...

CARDINAL: If envy were permitted a humble servant of God, I might be jealous of you, dear brother. So brief a voyage, gone but a week, and your wife's heart appears ready to break. Truly blessed is the man who is loved so ardently after seven years of marriage. Is it not seven years now, Countess?

COUNTESS: Our son is six now, yes.

COUNT: I shall bring back the first spring flowers from our wood.

COUNTESS: Will there ever be flowers? Will winter never end?

COUNT: Soon, my love, as always.

(The COUNT exits. A moment of silence as the CARDINAL and the COUNTESS are alone.)

CARDINAL: You wished to speak to me in private. A matter of the soul, Countess?

COUNTESS: Not now. My mind is unsettled.

CARDINAL: Were you at the ball last night?

COUNTESS: We stayed at home.

CARDINAL: I understand the Duke attended. He and several of his entourage wore the costume of a nun.

COUNTESS: Do you find that amusing?

CARDINAL: I am told he looked ravishing.

COUNTESS: Is there so little respect now for sacred things?

CARDINAL: One can respect the sacred and yet,
in a lighthearted moment, wear its mask. No harm
is intended.

COUNTESS: I know nothing of the Duke's intention.
I do know the example it sets. I find it revolting.

CARDINAL: Come, Countess. The Duke is young and
high-spirited.

COUNTESS: You, Cardinal, are one of those who place
words on an anvil and beat them into different shapes
until they mean what you please.

CARDINAL: You make too much of it. Your
condemnation outweighs the deed.

COUNTESS: How do you weigh the deed of murder?
His own half- brother poisoned, so he could seize the
throne for himself.

CARDINAL: Hearsay, Countess.

COUNTESS: Because no one dare bring charges.

CARDINAL: Why such hatred for the Duke? As a ruler,
he has proven to be both strong and politically adept.

COUNTESS: Your courtly politics are a mystery to me.
But instruct me, Your Holiness. As his chief advisor,
do you regret that the Duke of Florence is a puppet
of the Emperor Charles and a tool of the Pope? You,
my husband's brother—do you care that German
soldiers cast their shadows on the streets of your city?
Do you hear the cries of the people, Cardinal Cibo?
Or will you order the clergy to ring the church bells
and drown out the sound of their suffering?

(She exits. The CARDINAL *reflects silently a moment.
A servant boy,* AGNOLO, *enters, sees the* CARDINAL,
and bows. AGNOLO *starts to leave.)*

CARDINAL: The Countess is absent, Agnolo. You have a
letter for her. Give it to me.

(AGNOLO *hesitates.*)

CARDINAL: There can never be harm in obeying a priest of the church, Agnolo. Always remember that. Give me the letter.

(AGNOLO *does so.*)

CARDINAL: The perfect servant. Unable to speak or to write. You will go far, my son... (*He reads.*) "Countess, you will give yourself to me, or you bring ruin upon yourself and both our houses." The Duke lacks style, but no one can say he is indirect... Ah! Women are the great mystery, Agnolo. God alone can decipher their hearts. Here stood the countess, so convincingly tearful at her husband's farewell. Then so loudly condemning of the Duke—while silently she awaits his next declaration of love. Was it but a play, acted for my benefit? Which part was real, which a fabrication of the stage? ...Two months straight he has pursued her. A long time for Alessandro de Medici. It should be time enough for the countess.

CARDINAL: (*Handing back the letter to* AGNOLO) Deliver this to her. And trust in me.

(*He extends his hand;* AGNOLO *kisses his ring. They exit separately.*)

1.4

(*The Ducal Palace. Enter the* DUKE, *followed by* VALORI *and* SALVIATI.)

DUKE: What does your boss have to say, Valori?

VALORI: Sire, the Pope sends a thousand blessings to the Duke of Florence.

DUKE: That's all he sends me, blessings?

VALORI: And a complaint, sire.

DUKE: Ah.

VALORI: His Holiness fears that your rule over the city is too harsh and— how shall I say? —greedy. He reminds you that the Florentines are unused to absolute rule. They long for a return to their precious republic. The more oppressive your policies, the more you feed their discontent and invite them toward rebellion. The Emperor himself has expressed the same dissatisfaction with you.

DUKE: Salviati.

SALVIATI: Sire?

DUKE: *(Looking offstage)* What an extraordinary horse's ass I see in the courtyard. Is that your animal?

SALVIATI: It is, sire.

DUKE: Magnificent beast. And do you beat him?

SALVIATI: When I must, sire.

DUKE: Sir Envoy. An emperor and a pope saw fit to make of me a king. But it is I who have to rule the city. And I reply to your employer that if I must use my scepter to bloody this ancient animal into submission, so I shall. Anything more?

VALORI: One thing, sire. This matter of sanctuary.

DUKE: "Sanctuary"? Salviati, can you translate this man? I don't speak Pope.

SALVIATI: Lorenzo, sire.

DUKE: Lorenzaccio?

VALORI: Sire, if I may speak frankly.

DUKE: Could such a miracle occur? Let us witness it. *(He goes to the small table and pours himself some wine.)*

VALORI: His Holiness considers your cousin, Lord Lorenzo de Medici, a fugitive from justice.

DUKE: And his crime?

VALORI: Decapitation, sire.

DUKE: Do you hear that, Salviati? Little Lorenzo,
a cold-blooded executioner. 'Tis true, all true.
He chopped off the heads of a dozen men in broad
daylight. Oh, sordid crime! Did none of these brave
men fight back, Sir Envoy? Eh?

VALORI: None, sire.

DUKE: No. As they were made of stone, every one.
The Pope's precious statues in the Constantine Arch,
beheaded by the drunken Lorenzaccio.

VALORI: His Holiness cannot overlook such
debauchery, sire.

DUKE: Oh, the lessons your Pope could give us all in
debauchery! He can start with his own bastard son and
the boy's dear friend, the Bishop of Fano.

VALORI: Sire, it is known that Lorenzo is an atheist.

DUKE: God save the lad.

VALORI: And that you and he have appeared in public
seated upon the same horse.

DUKE: God save the horse.

VALORI: It is even rumored, sire, that you and he,
by cover of darkness, illicitly entered a holy convent.

DUKE: The "holy" I dispute.

VALORI: And further, that he ministers to your
pleasures at court. Some have even called him your...

DUKE: My pimp?

VALORI: That is one of the words that has been used,
sire.

DUKE: I begin to lose my sense of humor, Envoy.

(Enter the CARDINAL*)*

DUKE: Cardinal Cibo. Just in time to hear the latest from Rome. I am accused of harboring a dangerous criminal. Can you guess who it might be?

CARDINAL: Your cousin Lorenzo, sire. The Pope has denounced him publicly.

DUKE: Do you not find that comical?

CARDINAL: I find it a matter of serious concern, sire. Lorenzo may be more dangerous to you than you realize.

DUKE: Little Lorenzaccio, the greatest coward in Florence? A philosopher, a pathetic scratcher of bad verses who goes about the streets without a sword lest he be terrified by its shadow. Salviati, is this not madness?

SALVIATI: Sire, he's not to be trusted. He'd stab you in the back if he could profit from it.

DUKE: Lorenzaccio?

CARDINAL: Even this name you give him— "filthy Lorenzo" —he revels in the mockery of it. More distance between you, sire, is my counsel.

DUKE: Let me tell you something, Cibo. These plots against me by the banished families—it is "filthy Lorenzo" who informs me. He hears everything, knows all the darkest secrets. He has even befriended the Strozzis. You may call him my pimp and despise him for it, but I say this: I love Lorenzo de Medici, and he will remain here at court with me, and I will not have it otherwise.

(Enter LORENZO, *pulling on a boot. He limps across the room and lies down on the floor.)*

Gentlemen, behold: the topic of our debate. Note the sunken eyes, the ghostly pallor of a survivor of last night's ball.

LORENZO: Good day to you, my lords. It is day, is it not?

DUKE: How notorious you've become, dear cousin. Did you know the Pope wants to extradite you?

LORENZO: So early in the morning, my liege? Very unchristian of him.

DUKE: Valori?

VALORI: In the Christian spirit, sire, we would be willing to wait until after mid-day meal.

LORENZO: What's this? A man of wit, from the Vatican?

VALORI: Not all the Pope's men are made of stone, my lord.

DUKE: Salviati and the Cardinal here think you dangerous, cousin.

LORENZO: I, dangerous? (To the CARDINAL) Your Grace, you flatter me. (He goes to table, pours water in a small basin and sprinkles it on his face.)

CARDINAL: Highly unlikely, I assure you.

LORENZO: Dangerous to whom, sir? The ladies of the night or my cousin the Duke?

CARDINAL: Both, it may be, but I address myself to the latter.

LORENZO: And I undress myself to the former. I do confess it guiltily.

DUKE: A hit, gentlemen. En garde, Cibo.

LORENZO: But tell me, Your Grace, am I a threat to Alessandro's soul or to his person?

CARDINAL: Both, again, it may be.

LORENZO: But I know nothing of his soul. I could not locate it even with a map. Where resides the soul, dear Cardinal?

CARDINAL: That is a matter of speculation among scholars of the church.

LORENZO: Speculate with me, Your Grace. Where resides the soul?

CARDINAL: Within the lung, some say.

LORENZO: Not higher in the corpus?

CARDINAL: Higher, say others.

LORENZO: Not lower, then?

CARDINAL: Lower, say other scholars.

LORENZO: Well, if scholars will allow, as I have long suspected, that a man's soul may be found hanging between his legs, then it is all too true, I am a threat to the Duke's soul.

CARDINAL: This is an insult.

DUKE: You were right, Cibo. Lorenzo is a dangerous man when the battle is wits.

(LORENZO *goes to table and pours himself a drink.*)

SALVIATI: But a sorry woman of a man when the battle is swords.

LORENZO: Salviati. Is that you? I didn't see you. The bright sun imperiled my vision and made you quite invisible to me—sweet blindness of a moment.

SALVIATI: One so quick to laugh at others should be as quick to defend himself. (*He draws his sword.*)

VALORI: A drawn sword in the presence of the Duke!

LORENZO: You mistake me, sir.

DUKE: Go on, Lorenzo. Fight him.

LORENZO: I am no soldier, gentlemen, only a poor lover of philosophy.

SALVIATI: Your tongue is a weapon and a vile one. Defend yourself.

LORENZO: I have no sword.

DUKE: Take mine.

(He offers him a sword.)

LORENZO: Cousin, what are you saying? This is all in jest.

DUKE: No more. You disgrace the name of Medici. Take it.

(DUKE pushes LORENZO toward SALVIATI.)

LORENZO: Sire—

DUKE: I am a bastard, born of a kitchenmaid, yet I wear the family name with pride. While you, full-blooded though you are, tremble like a schoolboy when you are challenged. Fight him.

LORENZO: Alessandro—

DUKE: Behold him, all of you! Let the court and all the city witness this spectacle! O cowardice! There, I mark his face go pale, his knees grow weak—

(LORENZO faints, dropping the sword.)

VALORI: *(Going to him)* The poor young man.

DUKE: What did I tell you? Here lies the dangerous Lorenzaccio.

SALVIATI: I curse him as a coward and a worthless dog.

DUKE: Watch your tongue, Salviati. He is still my cousin.

VALORI: *(Getting him to his feet)* Let me help you, my lord.

DUKE: Have him brought home to his mother.

(LORENZO *and* VALORI *exit.*)

CARDINAL: Your Highness, surely you don't believe this masquerade.

DUKE: What am I not to believe?

CARDINAL: Fainting at the sight of a sword—it's play-acting.

DUKE: Would a Medici make a game of dishonoring himself publicly? No, I've seen it before. It's all too true.

(They exit.)

1.5

(Outside the walls of the city. MARIE, LORENZO's *mother, and* CATHERINE, *his sister.)*

CATHERINE: Look how beautiful the sky is at this hour, mother. And the hills, in this light. We used to take the air outside the city walls nearly every evening.

MARIE: It is no longer safe, outside these walls or within them.

CATHERINE: But at moments like this, I feel that God is everywhere, watching over us.

MARIE: I marvel that He is able to watch at all. How disheartened He must be at what He witnesses here below.

CATHERINE: So much has changed in so brief a time. Yet all may change again, and our city and our freedom be restored to us.

MARIE: It is a child's false hope.

CATHERINE: But hope, just the same. If we preserve only that, it can never be said that all has been taken from us.

MARIE: These worldly matters occupy you too much, Catherine. In the convent, you will be free of such worries. Why do you still delay your entry?

CATHERINE: God will show me when I am ready.

(Church bells ring.)

MARIE: It is time for us to return.

CATHERINE: Can we not stay a few moments longer?

MARIE: Night will be upon us.

CATHERINE: Mother. Something else is troubling you. Won't you tell me?

MARIE: This latest story about Lorenzo. All the city has heard it by now.

CATHERINE: Cowardice is not a crime. Nor is courage always a virtue.

MARIE: Could you love a coward, Catherine? What woman will want to take his arm, what man will shake his hand?

CATHERINE: I used to see a light in my brother's eyes. He had the fire of ambition inside him once. I see it still, for a moment, before it disappears. When I think of how he was as a child, so full of love. When he saw someone suffer, he was wounded by it. "That man is poor, sister, and that one is sick. How can we help them?" He was so beautiful then.

MARIE: The corruption in his heart has risen to his cheeks. His smile is gone, his face has the pallor of a corpse.

CATHERINE: There must be some goodness in him still. It can't all have been taken away.

MARIE: I dreamed once that he would be a ruler of Florence. It was in his blood. He had the learning. He had a love for the people and a sense of justice. But this

city has destroyed him, just as he has helped destroy
the city.

CATHERINE: The air has turned chill. Let us go back
now, mother. Shadows are moving. There are men on
the road.

MARIE: All the sons of the banished families. They were
once our friends. Now I am ashamed to look into their
eyes, for the hatred I see there. My own son betrayed
them to the Duke.

CATHERINE: Mother, no.

MARIE: He has tied himself to Alessandro, as to a stone,
and he leaps into the darkest waters, as though in
longing for his own destruction. In all Florence, only
Philip Strozzi remains his friend. I fear Lorenzo will
dishonor even that.

(They exit.)

2.1

(The DUKE's *bedroom. It is night. The* DUKE *sits on his bed. A* WOMAN *lies next to him, crying loudly into a pillow.)*

DUKE: Lorenzo!

(Enter LORENZO.*)*

DUKE: Must I scream out my lungs for you in my own palace? I ordered you to remain nearby me.

LORENZO: I was walking in the garden, sire, beneath your windows.

DUKE: Then you heard her?

*(*WOMAN *cries loudly.)*

LORENZO: Indistinctly, my lord.

DUKE: Such lamentation. Your actor at the guild fair is more credible. Must they all be drunken whores?

*(*DUKE *throws* WOMAN *out the door.)*

LORENZO: You insisted that she drink, my liege.

DUKE: But must she talk and talk?

*(*WOMAN *reenters, runs to* DUKE *and embraces him.)*

DUKE: Desire transforms upon the instant to disgust. Do you not mark it, cousin? Why is it so?

*(*DUKE *throws her out again.)*

LORENZO: Desire is an appetite like any other, and quickly sated.

*(*WOMAN *reenters and crawls across bed toward the* DUKE.*)*

DUKE: Then call me full and have her put out at the gate.

(DUKE *throws her gown to her.*)

LORENZO: In the dark of night?

DUKE: Let her stumble home to her husband, and pity the man his fate.

(LORENZO *carries* WOMAN *off.*)

DUKE: Where are my other guests?

LORENZO: Gone, my lord.

DUKE: All? They were eager enough to gorge themselves at my table.

LORENZO: They are felled by drink or the lateness of the hour.

DUKE: Call them back.

LORENZO: Now, my lord?

DUKE: They had not my permission to quit the royal presence. Have soldiers drag them from their beds and beat them if need be, but call them back.

LORENZO: As you wish, my lord. (*He starts to leave.*)

DUKE: As I wish. Everything is as I wish, and nothing. Lorenzaccio. My shoulders.

(LORENZO *kneels behind* DUKE *on bed and massages his shoulders, his neck.*)

Leave them in their beds. What need have I of false smiles and empty phrases? ...How delicate, your fingers... Why do you walk in my garden at midnight?

LORENZO: The moonlight draws dreams from certain plants. One has only to breathe them in, and they are yours.

DUKE: From what plants are nightmares drawn?
Name them, that I might have 'em torn out by the root.

LORENZO: Your sleep is troubled, sire.

DUKE: When it comes. You'll lie next to me tonight.
I will not be alone.

LORENZO: Only we two, my lord?

DUKE: Call Agnolo to us. For our comfort.

LORENZO: As you wish, my lord.

(Lights. Transition)

2.2

(The STROZZI *home. Enter* PHILIP STROZZI *carrying a book and thinking aloud: the earnest philosopher, trying to reason out the problems of humankind. As he speaks, his son* PIERO *and his daughter* LOUISA *arrive, but they are hesitant to interrupt.*

PHILIP: Corruption. Is it a law of nature? What we
call virtue—is it nothing more than a suit of clothes,
a costume we don for Sunday mass? The remaining
days we withdraw to our balconies and watch life pass
us by on the street below.

PIERO: Father.

(A gesture by PHILIP *to be silent until he has worked this out)*

PHILIP: And we, the old philosophers of the world,
what improvement have we made to men's souls in
four or five millennia? What right have I, Philip Strozzi,
to pass the years dying quietly among my books and
papers?

LOUISA: Father.

(Same gesture)

PHILIP: How easily the architect creates great palaces with nothing more than ink and a compass, and yet—he is helpless to lift even a single block of stone when the true work of building begins. Why does the philosopher survey the world around him when the tiniest insect that passes before his eye will blot out the sun entire.

PIERO: Father?

LOUISA: Father?

(PHILIP *sits at his desk.*)

PHILIP: Is man's happiness but an illusion? Is evil eternal, irrevocable, unchanging? No. For in a single phrase there is power to rouse the people, and philosophers too, from their torpor: the *republic* of Florence. Restoration of our laws, our rights, our dignity. *(He writes.)*

LOUISA: Father, ten more are banished from the city. Old Galazzeo.

PIERO: And poor Mafeo, his sister taken from her bed and corrupted in a single night.

LOUISA: It was Salviati. He boasted of it.

PIERO: He spoke to you? Salviati?

LOUISA: It was nothing. A passing comment, after the masked ball.

PIERO: What did he say?

LOUISA: It's not worthy of the re-telling, Piero.

PIERO: Tell me, worthy or no. The man is a villain. He spoke of my father?

LOUISA: No, Piero.

PIERO: Then he spoke of me. Tell me, Louisa, what insult he made, for he knows no other language.

PHILIP: My children. Please.

PIERO: Oh heaven, send me reason to cut off the man's ears! Tell me, sister, or my imagining will beggar truth. What did he say?

LOUISA: He followed me to a cloth merchant's stand.

PIERO: Followed you?

LOUISA: And declared his desire for me.

PIERO: His desire? For my sister?

LOUISA: I spurned and scolded him, as an honorable woman should. Then Lorenzo distracted him.

PIERO: Lorenzo! Another villain!

LOUISA: I left and found you, and we returned home. It is forgotten.

PIERO: Salviati...

LOUISA: I should not have told him, father, but for fear he would think it more than it is. I lend it no more importance than the barking of a dog.

PIERO: Oh I will teach this dog a lesson. I'll do it with my sword!

PHILIP: Piero, no. You were ever too hot-blooded. Let cooler reason govern you. Will a Salviati goad us to violence?

PIERO: Will he prove the Strozzis cowards that leave an insult unanswered?

PHILIP: The snake does not trouble the eagle. Let the serpent slither in the dust according to its nature and not drag the nobler creature down.

PIERO: Let noble creatures act their parts, father, or noble they cannot claim to be. When did Florence ever need us more?

PHILIP: I avow the need, but insist on the rule of reason. What is the hour?

LOUISA: The angelus has rung, father.

PHILIP: We go in to sup, my children, and put off all vengeful thought. Come, Piero, come, I do command it.

(PHILIP and LOUISA exit. PIERO hesitates for a moment and follows.)

2.3

(The interior of a great cathedral. VALORI, the papal envoy, and LORENZO. A young artist, TEBALDEO, sketches upstage and overhears their conversation.)

VALORI: Behold, sir, the splendor. What man could be unmoved by the glory of a great cathedral?

LORENZO: Is that why you bring me here, Valori?

VALORI: The harmonious sounds of the organ, the delicate voices of the choir. The magnificent paintings of the masters. Is it not splendid?

LORENZO: It is. And is not.

VALORI: Oh, it may seem excess to the enemies of pleasure, the tonsured monk, the grim parish priest. But I say there is nothing more admirable than a religion that would conquer souls through pure beauty. Is it not so, sir?

LORENZO: It is. And is not.

VALORI: Would any worthy priest wish to serve a vengeful God? Religion is no bird of prey, say I, but a dove that soars lovingly above the hearts and dreams of men. And here before us is proof. Is it not so, sir?

LORENZO: What you say is perfectly true and perfectly false, like all else in this world.

VALORI: I detect in you, Lord Lorenzo, a mind of quality. Yet that quality, I fear, is quite subverted by a troubled heart.

LORENZO: Your Pope knows me for a head-lopping atheist. Do you contradict him, Valori?

VALORI: I convey His Holiness's opinions, sir, but hold my own. I do not think you so corrupt as some do claim, or perhaps as you pretend.

(TEBALDEO, *who has overheard their conversation, steps forward; he carries a rolled canvas.*)

TEBALDEO: God be with you, father.

LORENZO: Who is this?

TEBALDEO: Forgive me, my lord, a humble artist who owes thanks to this priest for his words. To hear from your lips, father, what I feel so deeply in my heart-it is a great gift. (*Bows and starts to go.*)

VALORI: You are a painter, then?

TEBALDEO: (*Stopping*) I am, though I fear I am a better lover of art than a maker of it. Before the genius of Raphael and Buonarroti, I stand in awe. The choir sings to me the music of the masters' souls. In the house of God is revealed the full glory of the artist.

VALORI: You have a true artist's spirit. What is your name?

TEBALDEO: Tebaldeo, father.

VALORI: Bring some of your work to my residence. Perhaps I shall be your patron.

TEBALDEO: I am honored, father.

LORENZO: No, wait. Show us your work now. You hold a canvas. Is it yours?

(*Takes canvas from* TEBALDEO's *shoulder bag*)

TEBALDEO: Nothing more than a poor sketch of a rich dream, my lord.

LORENZO: You paint dreams? I would have some of mine sit for you.

(LORENZO *unrolls canvas and puts it on the floor.*)

TEBALDEO: What does an artist do, lord, if not paint dreams? The great masters painted theirs and the result is immortal. But alas, the dreams of a humbler talent must be watered with many bitter tears before they grow.

VALORI: In truth, this is very fine. And you are yet so young.

LORENZO: Is it landscape or portrait? How does it go-this way? Or this?

TEBALDEO: You mock me, my lord. It is a view of Campo Santo. *(He picks up canvas and puts it back in shoulder bag.)*

LORENZO: The burial ground? So there, you've painted something immortal. Was it hard?

VALORI: Don't tease him so, my lord. His eyes fill with tears at your jesting.

LORENZO: Come to my rooms, Tebaldeo. I'll have a famous courtesan pose for you in the nude.

TEBALDEO: I love my art too much to prostitute it, lord.

LORENZO: Your God took the trouble to make her. Surely you can take the trouble to paint her. Will you paint me a view of Florence, then?

TEBALDEO: I will, my lord.

LORENZO: From what angle?

TEBALDEO: From the east, lord, on the banks of the Arno.

LORENZO: You would paint Florence? Her houses, her streets?

TEBALDEO: Yes, my lord.

LORENZO: Then why will you not paint a prostitute if you will paint a city of whores?

TEBALDEO: I would never speak thus of my mother, lord.

LORENZO: If Florence is your mother, then I call you bastard.

VALORI: Lord Lorenzo, I beg you.

TEBALDEO: She has suffered a wound, my lord, it is true. But her drops of blood are precious and will one day cure all ills.

LORENZO: Let me play the alchemist and distill your meaning. The tears of the people fall as pearls, and in the suffering of a great city great heroes are born. Oh, admirable philosopher! Whole families are destroyed, a nation reduced to misery, and it stirs the little painter's imagination! And still you praise God?

TEBALDEO: I pity a people's suffering, but I say it has purpose. From battlefields where men are slain, full harvests of wheat will spring.

LORENZO: I would have my servant beat you bloody.

TEBALDEO: Why, my lord?

LORENZO: For being lame.

TEBALDEO: I am not lame, my lord.

LORENZO: If not lame, you are mad.

TEBALDEO: I am neither, lord.

LORENZO: Then why do you stay in a city where the lowest servant of a Medici can knock out your brain for a jest and never answer justice for it?

TEBALDEO: I carry a dagger, my lord.

LORENZO: And would you strike the Duke with it, if first he struck you? He makes sport of murder, you've heard it said.

TEBALDEO: I would be right to kill him if he struck at me, lord.

LORENZO: You dare say such words to me?

TEBALDEO: Why do you press me so, lord? I mean no harm. What can my life or death matter to anyone?

LORENZO: Are you for the republic, painter? Are you a patriot, or do you love the Duke?

TEBALDEO: I am an artist, lord, nothing more. I love my mother and my God.

LORENZO: May one or the other protect you, Tebaldeo. You are as honest a man as can be found in Florence. Call on me tomorrow. I want you to paint me a man's portrait.

(*Exit* LORENZO. *The two men watch him go, then they exit. Lights out.*)

2.4

(*Lights up on the* COUNTESS *and* CARDINAL. *We are in the cathedral. The* COUNTESS *kneels at the prie-dieu, rosary in hand.*)

CARDINAL: You have not told me all. Continue, Countess.

COUNTESS: There is nothing more, your grace.

CARDINAL: Speak, I urge you. We are alone, save for your God.

2.   31

COUNTESS: I confess to you that I have had doubts about my faith.

CARDINAL: Go on.

COUNTESS: I slandered the holy church, your grace.

CARDINAL: How?

COUNTESS: I declared that it is corrupt. That the Bishop of Fano and others like him have turned it into a place of debauchery.

CARDINAL: These are trifles. What more?

COUNTESS: I have said all, your grace.

CARDINAL: Go to the heart of the matter, Countess. Before God, tell me the truth.

(COUNTESS *stands, crossing herself.*)

COUNTESS: The truth is, Cardinal, I trust you not.

CARDINAL: I am your confessor.

COUNTESS: You are my relative, my husband's brother, and I trust you not.

CARDINAL: Your soul is troubled. Have you not received a proposal? One that threatens the fidelity you have sworn to your husband?

COUNTESS: How is it you know so much of what you should never know?

CARDINAL: How did you answer this proposal?

COUNTESS: As a woman of honor.

CARDINAL: Then you rejected it and refused all further correspondence.

COUNTESS: No.

CARDINAL: No?

COUNTESS: I agreed to a meeting.

CARDINAL: And what took place at this meeting?

(She turns away.)

CARDINAL: Confide in me, Ricarda.

COUNTESS: Nothing took place.

CARDINAL: Nothing? No secret vow, no stolen kiss?

COUNTESS: Am I one who would lie before God?

CARDINAL: Tell me what occurred.

COUNTESS: Why do you press me so? You seek to betray me to my husband. You would see me ruined.

CARDINAL: I would see you raised up, and Florence with you. I know that the man you saw secretly was Alessandro, Duke of Florence.

COUNTESS: You who claim to save men's souls— beware your own, Cardinal Cibo.

CARDINAL: Hear me, Ricarda. Your secret is known to me alone. The laws of God and man command my silence. Yet think on this: one who knows all can accomplish all. Convert opposition, guide endeavor to triumph, secure a future to outshine the much regretted past.

COUNTESS: You men of the church—there is ever something hidden behind the tapestry of your words.

CARDINAL: More plainly, then. The Duke is powerful. So too his desire for you. How high might rise a woman exalted in the coarse heart of a tyrant? How expertly slip off the armor of his brutishness and unclench his fist from the city's throat? Countess. Your influence can be great, your reward greater still.

COUNTESS: How would I employ such influence?

CARDINAL: Be guided by me in these complexities. High matters of court are not a woman's realm.

COUNTESS: You advise infidelity to my husband.

CARDINAL: Upon your conjugal honor, one blemish scarcely visible. A sin so small for a cause so great.

COUNTESS: Whose cause? That of Florence or of Cardinal Cibo?

CARDINAL: You doubt me, then.

COUNTESS: That you are no patriot to any cause but your own, this I do not doubt. Your ambition is strong, but your position weak. Alessandro will not whisper in Cibo's ear, nor embrace his counsel, not stroll with him in the garden and unveil precious strategy. But Alessandro might do so willingly with a woman he desires, is it not so?

CARDINAL: If that woman is you.

COUNTESS: That you would use me to gain power for yourself, this too I do not doubt.

CARDINAL: The true advantage for Florence lies with me. With your aid, I can guide Alessandro back toward the rule of law, restore certain rights to the citizenry.

COUNTESS: I, who am so unschooled in politics, shall I tell you the strategy? When you can whisper to the emperor and the pope that Alessandro is ruled by the countess, and the countess by Cibo, then you shall have earned your reward.

CARDINAL: Florence, freed.

COUNTESS: Cibo to the Vatican, and the Vatican to Cibo.

CARDINAL: If ever I were so blessed to be named pope, think what advantage might then be yours. Ally with me, Ricarda, and see both our fortunes rise.

COUNTESS: But for this, your grace: I trust you not.

CARDINAL: Take yourself a shield, Countess. Make certain of its perfection and strength. One who would dare stand against me will need an armor impregnable. *(He exits.)*

COUNTESS: To divine this priest, I have not the wisdom. To counter him, I have not the power. He would gain his prize on the ruin of my honor... Now Alessandro presses me, and like an unskilled swordsman, I am cornered by my own maneuver. To play the lover and save the city. To touch this tyrant's heart, and waken some nobler element within, so that Florence might at last be freed. But the darker truth is... my own heart welcomes Alessandro's advance. Even desires it. I do not love him, I am sure of it. Something baser drives me to this. Marcelo, why are you gone now from Florence?

(Enter AGNOLO.)

COUNTESS: Agnolo?

(He bows)

COUNTESS: The Duke?

(He gestures offstage. COUNTESS hesitates, then walks off in the direction AGNOLO indicates. AGNOLO follows.)

2.5

(The home of LORENZO's mother. MARIE sits at the table as LORENZO paces. Enter his sister CATHERINE with tea and cups on a platter.)

CATHERINE: Lorenzo, you pace as if pursued. Will you not sit awhile and read to us, as you once did?

LORENZO: I read to you? It must have been in happier days, my sister, for all such time has vanished from my memory, as happiness from our lives. *(Sits.)*

MARIE: Are you not the author of your own unhappiness, my Lorenzo?

LORENZO: Multiple volumes, mother, in poetry and prose, to rival the libraries of the learned.

CATHERINE: Read to us from the ancient Roman histories, Lorenzo.

(CATHERINE *gets a book and gives it to* LORENZO.)

MARIE: Read us the story of Brutus.

CATHERINE: The most courageous man in Rome, you called him, for he struck against the tyrant to save the republic.

LORENZO: Fairy tales full of madmen. (*Grabs the book and throws it on the table*)

CATHERINE: How so?

LORENZO: Brutus was mad. He thought to cheat Caesar in the marketplace. But the price for a life is a life, so he was mad to think he could strike and strike a bargain too.

MARIE: I had a dream about you last night, my son.

LORENZO: A dream?

MARIE: More than a dream. A vision. I sat here, alone. The night was black and starless, a single candle lit the room. My thoughts were of you, in youth, a time when I was happy still. I heard footsteps echo in the hall. I turned and saw a man enter, dressed in black, a book under his arm. It was you, Lorenzo. "You have come back to me," I said, but the reply was silence. There came a chill into the room as if from an open vault, and when you moved to the chair by the window, I saw that you cast no shadow.

LORENZO: You saw this, mother?

MARIE: As I see you now.

LORENZO: My ghost.

CATHERINE: Lorenzo, you tremble from head to toe. It was only a dream.

LORENZO: Mother, watch again for the specter tonight, and if he returns, tell him... tell him that I will soon amaze him more fully than he now amazes me.

(*Enter two men,* BINDO *and* VENTURI.)

MARIE: Lorenzo. Your good cousin and uncle have asked to meet with you.

LORENZO: Bindo and Venturi? I was not told of your visit.

MARIE: We leave you now.

(*Exit* MARIE *and* CATHERINE.)

BINDO: Lorenzo. Why do you not deny the scandalous story they tell of you?

LORENZO: Which one, uncle? I am hard pressed to catalogue them all.

BINDO: That in the Duke's presence you were challenged and you fainted at the sight of a sword.

LORENZO: Ah, that one.

BINDO: In Rome I saw you use a sword, and skillfully. But here, as you live a vile life worthy of a dog, I am not surprised that you act like one.

LORENZO: The story is true, I fainted. Cousin Venturi, how is business? I understand sales have picked up since the Duke became your client.

BINDO: The Duke?

VENTURI: Sir, I am an importer of fine silk, in quantity. I am no merchant.

LORENZO: Yes, yes, I had forgotten. As merchant to the merchants you are no merchant but a philosopher of commerce.

BINDO: Your cousin is a patriot, Lorenzo—even though apparently he does business with the Duke?

VENTURI: I have never personally done business with the Duke.

BINDO: And whatever may be said of him, he does not faint at swords.

VENTURI: I am a sworn hater of the Duke, and his money.

BINDO: There are many of us still in this city who know Alessandro for what he is, and despise him for it. We will not sit idle while he builds his power on the ruins of our privilege. His German mercenaries daily become more lawless and violent. You were once a man of integrity, Lorenzo, a lover of liberty. If we take action, do you stand with us and with Florence? Or do you stand with Alessandro? Are you patriot or traitor? These questions we charge you to answer.

LORENZO: Cousin Venturi.

VENTURI: Sir?

LORENZO: Speak.

VENTURI: Speak, sir?

LORENZO: Quickly, while my uncle catches his breath or your chance is lost. Speak.

VENTURI: I never took a single coin from the Duke's hand.

LORENZO: I know you, sir, for the honest merchant you are not.

BINDO: Enough of your insolence. Answer me or be counted our enemy.

LORENZO: I am one of you, Uncle, from head to toe. Do you not see that I wear the hairstyle of freedom? And I dress in the fashion of the Florentine patriot, unto my most intimate garments.

(Enter CATHERINE, *veiled.)*

CATHERINE: Lorenzo. The Duke.

(The DUKE *enters.* CATHERINE *bows and exits quickly.)*

LORENZO: My lord. You do me honor to visit me in my mother's house.

DUKE: I have to speak with you. Who are these men?

LORENZO: Your highness, I present to you my uncle, Bindo Altoviti, just returned from a voyage to Naples or he would have come sooner to kneel at your feet. And this, lord, is the illustrious Baptista Venturi, importer of silk who will not sell you the slightest handkerchief.

DUKE: *(To* VENTURI*)* Do I know you?

VENTURI: No, your lordship!

DUKE: You sold me some silk—overpriced, as I recall.

VENTURI: Not I, my lord!

LORENZO: Let not the presence of royalty frighten you, my friends. All that you ask will be granted you by this great prince or let it be said evermore that Lorenzo's word has no credit with the Duke of Florence.

DUKE: Very well, then. What is it you ask, Bindo?

LORENZO: Bindo?

BINDO: Your highness, I don't know what to say.

LORENZO: The post of ambassador to Rome is presently vacant, my lord, and good Bindo deserves it above any man in Florence, so great is his attention to the house of Medici.

DUKE: In truth, Lorenzaccio? Then so be it. The ambassadorship is yours. Come tomorrow to the palace.

BINDO: No, but how can I possibly—?

LORENZO: Repay you.

BINDO: Repay you.

LORENZO: And for the worthy Venturi, my prince, though he will sell you no silk, none, yet would he have the royal privilege on flags and coats of arms throughout the city entire.

DUKE: All the city?

LORENZO: Grant this, my lord, or say that Alessandro does not love those who love him.

DUKE: Very well, very well. Are we through? Gentlemen, leave us, we have business to discuss.

VENTURI: Your royal graciousness— All the flags and coats of arms—I am overcome with joy—!

(VENTURI *bows many times as* LORENZO *leads him and* BINDO *out.*)

DUKE: I come to amaze you with news, my little Lorenzaccio.

LORENZO: Amaze me, my liege.

DUKE: She is mine. I had her last night for the first time.

LORENZO: Wondrous, my lord. Who?

DUKE: The countess, dear fool, who else?

LORENZO: Is it so?

DUKE: And you, who said she would not fall. How little you know women.

LORENZO: Too true. A little is perhaps all a man can know. Was she willing, lord?

DUKE: They are always willing, when they are done acting their scene of unwillingness.

LORENZO: So it is the same with all of them.

DUKE: Some play the scene longer, some more convincingly. But this one. What a wellspring of passion beneath that crystalline perfection. I was near swept away.

LORENZO: I am pleased for you.

DUKE: Lorenzo, brave knight! Why the melancholy face? Have you seen a sword waving about? Come drink with me. We'll talk of horses and women and popes, in descending order of esteem. In truth, Lorenzaccio, I have no friend but you. Yours are the only two eyes in all Florence that see me without reproach. At court I am surrounded by sniffling beggars and smiling plotters. The weak hate me for my power, the powerful hate me that I am not weak, and there's not a one of them knows a good bawdy story at the bottom of a cup. The palace stinks of ceremony and deceit. Escape with me, sweet cousin, to some unlikely tavern. We'll go in disguise, befoul our brains with drink, then jump upon the lowliest, onion-breathed whores that ever lifted skirts. Your sovereign commands you.

LORENZO: I may not, my prince. I am engaged.

DUKE: At what?

LORENZO: Your work, my lord. I dine with Philip Strozzi.

DUKE: That prattling old fool?

LORENZO: I have word that he opens his purse to every far cousin and stable boy of the banished families. I go to warn him of your displeasure, and listen at table for the crumbs of plots and policies against you.

DUKE: But must you go now?

LORENZO: While I have the appetite for it, my lord.

DUKE: At table with the Strozzis. Yet how is it they trust you, cousin? They know you are my intimate.

LORENZO: You forget, I am an expert player. I wear the mask of sympathy, the costume of friendship. I shed a tear of sorrow, as the part requires. To stare a man in the eye and lie to his face, my lord, is an art. I am an artist. You are a king, too earnest to master my skills.

DUKE: It may be so.

LORENZO: Feint of heart, sire, as you accuse me.

DUKE: Feint, as the swordsman, yes. Ah, Lorenzo. Without you, Florence would be a dungeon too dreary.

LORENZO: My lord: you recall that you wanted your portrait done. I have found you a young painter, a protégé of mine. Grant that I may send him to you.

DUKE: Yes, so be it.

(*Enter* CATHERINE, *unveiled, to clear the table. She sees the* DUKE *and gasps in surprise.*)

CATHERINE: Your highness, forgive me. I did not know you were present still.

DUKE: It is forgiven, my lady.

(*She bows and exits.*)

DUKE: Who, pray, was that, cousin?

LORENZO: No one, lord. A neighbor.

DUKE: Not so, not so. She resembles you. I dare say that was your sister. Are you hiding things from your Duke?

LORENZO: She is of no interest to you, lord.

DUKE: No interest? With those eyes? Arrange a *rendez-vous.*

LORENZO: Sire, she is virtuous. And worse, well
instructed in Latin, which she quotes endlessly.
She would drive you mad in an hour.

DUKE: No, no, that's a madness I welcome, even were it
seasoned with Cicero. Arrange it. What's yours is mine,
when and where I say. *(He exits.)*

2.6

(The STROZZI *home. Enter* PHILIP, *followed by* LOUISA.*)*

PHILIP: An insult. A reprisal. Kill and be killed.
Vengeance, that ancient story. Children walk beside
the caskets of their fathers, hatred takes root, and
whole generations spring from the earth, sword in
hand, to continue the bloodshed.

LOUISA: I was wrong to tell Piero of the insult, father.
I am to blame.

PHILIP: An insult from a man like Salviati. Will an
obscenity scribbled on our gates make us tear down
our house?

LOUISA: The wildness in my brother's eyes when he left
here. It frightened me so.

PHILIP: If he finds Salviati, the streets of Florence will
drink blood tonight. Once the appetite is wakened in
those ancient stones, they will drink long and deep.

LOUISA: But the city is dark, father, and there are so
many streets. Perhaps Piero is on his way home to us,
even now.

PHILIP: We will pay for his revenge with our freedom,
Louisa. Or what remains of it.

(Enter PIERO, *out of breath, with blood stains on his clothes.)*

PIERO: Our honor is defended.

LOUISA: Oh Piero! There is blood on your clothes.

PHILIP: My son. Are you wounded?

PIERO: The deed is done. Salviati is dead. We waited for him in the shadows. One of us stopped his horse, another struck him in the leg. And I—I delivered a blow to his head.

LOUISA: Piero, the look on your face. You terrify me.

(*Enter* LORENZO.)

LORENZO: It is a beautiful face. The face of vengeance.

PHILIP: Lorenzo.

PIERO: Why have you come here? No traitor will disgrace my father's house.

PHILIP: I shall determine who is guest and who a disgrace in my house. You are welcome, Lorenzo.

PIERO: Welcome like the pox.

PHILIP: Piero!

PIERO: I could toss him through that window and count the day a double triumph, for two vermin less in Florence.

PHILIP: Enough! This is the transformation vengeance enacts upon the soul. Lorenzo de Medici has never harmed this family. He has been friend to us in the past and I will have him treated as a friend now. As for you, Piero—either you were mad to do this bloody act, or the act has made you mad. Our task now is to hide you.

PIERO: I will not hide, father. I will walk the streets of Florence with my sword drawn and proclaim my deed to all the world.

PHILIP: No, it is to beg for further bloodshed.

PIERO: Our family was openly insulted, and I have openly defended our honor. In the name of God, how may that be wrong?

PHILIP: Oh, Piero. Come with me. Let us wash the blood from your hands. You are not wounded, my son?

(They exit.)

LORENZO: Louisa. Tell me. A blow to the head, did he say? Where have they taken the body?

LOUISA: Oh Lorenzo, how can you ask me such questions? How cruel we have become, all of us.

LORENZO: Louisa—

LOIUSA: Will you take this news to your Duke and betray us all?

(They exit separately.)

2.7

(DUKE at his palace, posing for his portrait by the painter TEBALDEO.)

DUKE: So many battles fought because of God. But none can be fought by him. Better a sharp blade than a dull prayer. The arm that raises the sword and brings it down upon the neck of our victim, it is a human arm of blood and bone. There is no God to it. The choice to kill is ours.

TEBALDEO: Be still, my lord, I beg you.

DUKE: How many men have these two hands sent back to their God? Can you guess?

TEBALDEO: I know not, my lord.

DUKE: Do you see the indelible stains of blood, as I do, seeped into the very skin? Will you dare paint these hateful weapons red, artist?

TEBALDEO: No, my lord.

DUKE: Then you lie with your brush. A ruler sleeps with death, his one faithful concubine. There is ever a cruelty necessary to power. I suspect that your God knows this infinitely well. *(A beat)* What is wrong, artist? Your hand is shaking.

TEBALDEO: It is nothing, highness.

DUKE: You're trembling. Does our discussion upset you?

TEBALDEO: I am unused to such topics, your highness.

DUKE: How can you paint humanity in all its sordid glory if you have no knowledge of its blacker colors? Answer me that, artist.

TEBALDEO: It would be quite impossible, my lord.

DUKE: There are no sainted painters. No Saint Raphaelo, no Saint Michelangelo, eh? You see my point?

TEBALDEO: Yes, your highness.

DUKE: The artist needs to wallow in the mud like the beggar, or the drunkard.

TEBALDEO: Yes, your highness. *(A beat)* Although...

DUKE: What.

TEBALDEO: I believe that the holy spirit graces all art worthy of the name. What I lack in knowledge I pray may be provided me from a divine source.

(Enter LORENZO.*)*

LORENZO: My lord. How goes your portrait? Are you pleased with my young protégé?

DUKE: He threatens to add the holy spirit to my picture. I will be unrecognizable.

LORENZO: You pose in the ancient Roman fashion, my lord. Naked to the waist.

DUKE: His idea.

LORENZO: I suggested it. A style worthy of your place in history.

DUKE: What is this? Flattery from my Lorenzo?

(LORENZO *takes the* DUKE's *body armor, an undercoat of fine steel mesh, from a table.*)

LORENZO: I have never seen you without your armor, Sir Knight. Do you wear it always?

DUKE: I am never without it.

LORENZO: It is very finely crafted.

DUKE: The finest in Europe.

LORENZO: But a strong blade could penetrate it, surely?

DUKE: There is none made by man that can pierce it. I was just telling your artist here about the necessities of rule. The royal person is ever a target.

LORENZO: It cannot be so everywhere, my lord.

DUKE: Can it not? Power gives birth to envy. The weaker the man, the more resentful he is of the throne until he thinks himself worthier to sit upon it than the lawful king.

LORENZO: And so the weak man dreams of murdering kings, my lord?

DUKE: And therein lies my defense, more certain than my coat of mail. Men are cowards, Lorenzaccio. They dream the night through of action, but on waking, they make water in their chamber pots and call for breakfast, which history will count the pinnacle of their day's accomplishments.

LORENZO: If men are such cowards, my liege, why then this armor?

DUKE: Because men are also mad, cousin. And I am cautious.

TEBALDEO: May I speak, your highness?

DUKE: If you must.

TEBALDEO: Resentment need never be the response to rule, if the rule is just.

DUKE: In whose eye, just?

TEBALDEO: God's eye, your highness.

LORENZO: There you have it, Sir Prince. Be more just before God, and let the people shower you with kisses.

DUKE: This is why we pay artists to paint and not to speak. Would God see it just if, upon suspicion, I strike down my enemy before he has the chance to strike me?

TEBALDEO: I think not, my lord.

DUKE: Strike first. This is ever how rulers remain in power. Is it not so, cousin?

LORENZO: It is, my prince.

DUKE: And if I rule, surely it is God's will, or would he not strike me down?

TEBALDEO: God's will is unknowable to such mortals as we, my lord.

DUKE: You see where this worn path leads, Lorenzo. Back on itself in a tired circle. Tell me, artist: Who is the man most despised in all of Florence? Who is he? You don't know? Answer, Lorenzo.

LORENZO: It is you, sire.

DUKE: Alessandro, Duke of Florence. The target of
threats and plots of every kind. Do you think it pleases
me to be an object of hatred? Oh, I would be adored.
What man does not wish it? I even long for it. Did you
know that about me, cousin? But I must first be obeyed.
I do not rule by nature or by popular consent. Power
has decreed that I shall hold power. I, the bastard
Alessandro, with the blood of a cousin on these newly
royal hands. If I loosen my grip, appease the people,
I will receive a knife in my back as thanks. I can tell you
this about rule: once you have been raised up, the peak
scaled, there is no safe descent. *(A beat)* Enough of this
portrait.

(Enter SALVIATI, *wounded, supported by* ATTENDANTS.*)*

SALVIATI: Alessandro, Duke of Florence!

DUKE: Salviati.

SALVIATI: These wounds I bear are yours. This attack
upon me is aimed at you.

DUKE: Call physicians! Who has done this? Name him!

SALVIATI: Piero Strozzi.

DUKE: Carry this man to my bed.

(As they exit, supporting SALVIATI*)*

DUKE: Summon my guard. I want Piero Strozzi
arrested. I will hang him in the morning.

(The DUKE *exits.)*

TEBALDEO: *(Seeing the* DUKE *has forgotten it)* His armor.

LORENZO: *(Taking it from him)* I'll see to it, little painter

(Lights)

2.8

(*The* STROZZI *palace*. PHILIP *and* PIERO.

PIERO: He feigned his death, the coward. One blow more and I could have earned the love of every Florentine patriot. I've let the moment slip from my grasp.

PHILIP: Two mounts are being readied. One of my servants will ride with you.

PIERO: But why should I flee and look the coward? I was right to strike him down.

PHILIP: Alessandro has ordered your arrest. If you fall into his hands, he can hang you, and I have no power to prevent it. Go, Piero, tonight toward Venice, where there are friends to shelter you.

PIERO: I will not, father.

PHILIP: Piero, I beg you—

PIERO: An avalanche begins with a single stone smaller than my fist. I start with fifty men, then a hundred, then a hundred more. I shall raise an army.

PHILIP: Oh children who play at soldier! Will you talk of life and death as though it were a game of cards? A rebellion, Piero—how many heads have turned gray reasoning out the consequence? How many lay at the executioner's feet? These are matters that frighten heaven itself. When you have overturned what is, what will you build in its place?

PIERO: The Medicis are the disease upon my city. The blade of a sword will cut out this tumor and cure us all to freedom once again.

PHILIP: It is not a cure but murder you propose.

PIERO: Join us, father. Every true Florentine will rally to the name of Philip Strozzi. Come, and see your dreams made real.

PHILIP: My dreams are for a republic and peace.

PIERO: Only blood will make that peace now.

PHILIP: No! No, I fear—for the lives of my children, the children of my fellow citizens.

PIERO: Then I act alone. You remain here among your books.

PHILIP: Piero—

PIERO: I retreat to the cellars and secret places of our friends. From the shadows I plot for light. I shall send word in a few days' time. We need you, father.

(PIERO *exits. After a moment,* LOUISA *enters.*)

LOUISA: How hollow and chill my brother's parting embrace did feel. I am full of dread at this farewell.

PHILIP: My indecision is a venom to me, Louisa, that poisons my reason. To do nothing were perhaps as cursed as choose the wrong course.

LOUISA: You must do as your conscience tells you. My mother would have expected no less.

PHILIP: I thank heaven she is not alive to witness these things.

LOUISA: Father. Someone warned you about the Duke and saved Piero from hanging. Who was it?

PHILIP: One whose throat our hot-blooded Piero longs to cut. It was Lorenzo.

(*They exit.*)

2.9

(LORENZO, *in his bedroom, with a servant,* SCORON.
They are engaged, it seems, in mortal combat. LORENZOhas
a dagger; SCORON *is unarmed but tries to defend himself
against the attack. During the fight,* LORENZO *seizes a chair,
tossing it violently about the room, which serves to increase
the general racket.*)

LORENZO: Die, die, die! You bastard, die!

SCORON: Assassin! Help!

LORENZO: Die, you butcher!

SCORON: Call for the guards!

LORENZO: Take this! And this!

SCORON: No! No!

LORENZO: Die now for every life you took!

SCORON: Murder!

LORENZO: Every family you destroyed!

SCORON: Assassin!

LORENZO: Smile for the demon come to take your soul!

SCORON: Help me! Murder!

LORENZO: To hell now, villain! Die!

(LORENZO *delivers the mortal blow; his rival falls a last time
to the floor and is motionless. A long beat.* LORENZO, *seated
on the floor, panting. Then* SCORON *raises his head.*)

SCORON: Are we done?

(LORENZO *nods.* SCORON *gets up.*)

SCORON: Same time tomorrow night?

(LORENZO *shakes his head.*)

SCORON: No? These are strange games you play, master.

LORENZO: You're well paid for them, Scoron, are you not?

SCORON: Full well, master.

LORENZO: Then you have no complaint.

SCORON: None, sir. Though I wonder at your neighbors. You rage in the dead of night like some hellish beast. They don't bang at your door or knock on your walls?

LORENZO: No longer. Now it's only poor mad Lorenzo, drunk again, playing at swords.

SCORON: Night after night, for near a month?

LORENZO: Curse him for a disturber of peaceful sleep, an assassin of dreams! And having sworn at me, they roll over and return to sleep. No one rises from his bed and throws open his shutters. None gather in the courtyard to stare up at my rooms.

(LORENZO *gives* SCORON *a bag of money.*)

SCORON: They are used to it, then.

LORENZO: I could cut the throats of thirty men in my bedroom, drag their bodies down the stairs, and no neighbor would so much as open his door. It is only mad Lorenzo, a coward who frightens sleep, for he has not the courage to frighten men.

SCORON: There's a purpose to your play, my lord. You have an enemy. Tell me who he is, and let me see to him.

LORENZO: I have an enemy, Scoron, yes. But the seeing to it is my task alone.

SCORON: Just say the word. I'd nail Christ back up on his cross, if you asked me.

LORENZO: My thanks to you, good friend. Go now.

(Exit SCORON*)*

(Alone on his bed) I have an enemy, yes. I desire his
death so strongly, it burns me to the very bone. There
is a savagery in me. What beast invaded my mother's
dreams when she carried me in her womb? For in truth
what harm has my enemy done to me? In his manner,
has he not been good to me? Does he not declare his
love for me? What kind of man am I? None, it may be,
but an instrument of heaven, called to fulfill the divine
will on earth, then fade away forgotten.... A sign sent
to me last night, a comet in the Eastern sky. Is my task
then not divinely clear? To kill a king. To murder
Alessandro, Duke of Florence. Alone, here, in this
my little room. To stain bed and walls and all forever
crimson with a cousin's blood. I, the most notable
coward in Florence... A vision haunts me: Alessandro
stands before me. The hour sounds. I draw my dagger,
and it ignites in my assassin's hand like the flaming
sword of the avenging angel. I am consumed in fire and
never strike my prey, but float harmless down as softest
ash upon him.... But no. I am chosen, my hour is come.
I take me now the hero's role of Brutus and cut this
Caesar down. I carve my name in the hearts and history
of my time. Lorenzo de Medici, the man who saved
Florence.

(Lights)

(Intermission)

3.1

(A street in Florence)

PHILIP: Justice! I call upon you, citizens, for justice!

LOUISA: Father, come in doors, I beg you.

PHILIP: Whose doors, Louisa? These that belonged to my father, and his father before him? Can the Duke of Florence seize them for his own?

LOUISA: Father, please.

PHILIP: I stand here on these streets a week, a month, a year if I must until I have justice.

LOUISA: We must send word to Piero. We have so little time.

PHILIP: My own son, condemned to death by royal decree. I am ordered to surrender him—my own flesh—or surrender my ancestral home. Philip Strozzi, banished? The oldest and noblest family of Florence, exiled by a bastard ruler. Can heaven be indifferent to this outrage?

LOUISA: Let us ally ourselves with trusted friends, the other banished families, then join in Piero's call to arms.

PHILIP: I counseled Piero against reprisal. I urged reason, my oldest and truest ally. There were words of peace upon these lips, Louisa, but see now the bitter draught I am made to swallow.

LOUISA: We must take action, father.

PHILIP: But what action? And how?

(Enter LORENZO.*)*

LORENZO: Does Philip Strozzi beg alms on the streets of Florence?

PHILIP: I beg the alms of justice.

LOUISA: Lorenzo, help us. Piero is condemned to death, my father threatened with banishment.

LORENZO: Yes, I know.

LOUISA: Can you stand by and watch an old man so pure of heart suffer these wrongs?

LORENZO: Tell me what you want of me.

LOUISA: To take action. To help us.

LORENZO: To do what?

LOUISA: To overturn the citadel where the coward Alessandro hides, throw its stones into the river, and him with it!

PHILIP: Louisa, no!

LORENZO: I shall help you, my dearest friends, in this way: I advise you. Do nothing.

LOUISA: Nothing?

LORENZO: Or better still, leave Florence.

LOUISA: This is your advice to us?

PHILIP: That I should end my days an exile, and die in some roadside inn?

LORENZO: Do as I advise you.

LOUISA: We called you by the sacred name of friend. We made ourselves deaf to the insults against you, blind to your deeds. The shadow of your reputation fell across the honor of our family, and still we welcomed you. When men called you leper, when my own brother cursed you, I spoke for you, the Lorenzo I played with as a child, generous of heart, and wise, the boy who had a poet's soul. I loved you once.

LORENZO: Louisa—

LOUISA: But now I see the corruption in that soul. Lorenzo is dead. In his place, we have this vile ghost who knows not honor or friendship or courage. I am sick at the sight of him. *(She exits.)*

PHILIP: You once told me that the true Lorenzo hides behind the mask. If there is something honest in you still, show it me now. Let the actor unmask the man, and speak true.

LORENZO: Go home, my lord.

PHILIP: No. I go to the homes of patriots. We will band together and call for the rule of law and reason.

LORENZO: Reason has been subverted. The law resides in me.

PHILIP: What do these words mean?

LORENZO: Your son's life is in danger, your home and family threatened.

PHILIP: And I desire their salvation, all.

LORENZO: And you will have it—if you do nothing.

PHILIP: I grow angry trying to understand you. Declare who and what you are!

LORENZO: I am an instrument of God, precious as gold.

PHILIP: Enough of this game!

LORENZO: Gold, say I! For I shall murder Alessandro.

PHILIP: What? You?

LORENZO: Go home, Philip.

PHILIP: Lorenzo—

LORENZO: Fear not for Piero, or for your estate. Take no action, I warn you. For in two days' time, Alessandro de Medici will exist no more.

PHILIP: Is this some madness? Alessandro, murdered. You amaze me, Lorenzo. And you frighten me. What have you become?

LORENZO: You knew me, Philip, when I was virtuous. I believed in the glory of mankind, as a martyr believes in his God. Twenty years of study was my life, the reading of the great authors. Then one night, I sat alone in the ancient coliseum at Rome. From out of the darkness, a spirit came upon me. It flew past and touched my hair, as light as a breath of wind, and I was doomed. Until that moment, I was at peace. I was good, Philip, in heart and deed. But now, to my eternal despair, I wanted to be great. A Brutus to the Caesars of the world. I swore that night that I, Lorenzo de Medici, would come face to face with tyranny and kill it with my own hand.

PHILIP: Beware pride, Lorenzo. You have suffered some delusion, a dream too vivid. You are no assassin.

LORENZO: The task became my one goal and sole excuse for living. Alessandro became my prey, and I his trusted friend. An army of a thousand men could not get within a mile of the Duke of Florence without bloody combat. But I walked at his side, flattered him, professed to love him, tasted upon his very lips the dregs of his own debauchery.

PHILIP: I read the shame in your face to recall these things.

LORENZO: To capture my prey, I became as he. Cowardly, depraved. Steeped in lechery and disgrace.

PHILIP: It was your mask.

LORENZO: Was it? Murder of the innocent, defilement of the pure. Hope and goodness ground into sorrow. I was witness and partner to these acts.

PHILIP: The fault lay with Alessandro.

LORENZO: But I bear the wound. I see men now for what they are, no longer what I wish them to be. Human nature, Philip—I found her in the darkened alleyways, she lifted her skirts and pulled me down. And I exulted in it. Now I know. It is a foul and sordid business, life, and I am infected by it, incurably.

PHILIP: You despair beyond all reason. There is evil in men, yes, but not without some good, as no shadow exists but for the light.

LORENZO: Noble Philip. You have lived like a beacon on the shore. In the waters you see the reflection of your own goodness. But I plunged into the depths, found the shipwrecks, the human skulls, the monstrous Leviathans that crawl in the mud below. You wish to know why I murder my cousin? Because I am sick at the sight of men. Because I am sick at the braying sound of their prayers, because their stench poisons the bread I eat. Every nameless coward in Florence vilifies me and slanders my name. I will answer in blood. It is time for the world to know who I am. I kill because murder is all that remains now of my honor. I kill to prove that I am still alive.

PHILIP: The violence in your words, Lorenzo—

LORENZO: And in my heart.

PHILIP: Murder resolves nothing, blood engenders blood. Would you throw away your own life to take another's?

LORENZO: When I murder my cousin, the city will be free for the taking. Your banished families need only rise up, act with courage, and bring to birth the finest republic ever seen in Europe. This is my gift to Florence.

PHILIP: No true republic can be founded upon a crime. Give up this enterprise, Lorenzo.

LORENZO: I can not. It may be some spirit of heaven that summoned me to it.

PHILIP: There is nothing in heaven, or on this earth, that requires this act of you.

LORENZO: I am chosen.

PHILIP: For murder?

LORENZO: For the execution of a tyrant.

PHILIP: Then a demon spirit called you, if spirit it was.

LORENZO: I would be a Brutus.

PHILIP: If you dream of glory and a bronze statue in the city square, awaken Lorenzo. The story of Brutus ends in suicide and defeat. You have not the nature, nor in truth the courage for this act.

LORENZO: I stand on Alessandro's corpse and toss a coin. Heads, I am a savior. Tails, a murderer. The difference is no more than the thickness of a coin. Let men judge me as they will-but not forget me. *(He kisses* PHILIP's *cheek, a gesture of farewell.)* Keep my secret until the deed is done. *(He exits.)*

3.2

*(*CATHERINE *at her home)*

CATHERINE: *(Reading a letter)* "I know that your brother has spoken to you of me. But he cannot have captured in mere words my true desire for you. Let this letter express what my lips cannot yet whisper in your ear—that my heart bleeds for you. Until our *rendez-vous.* Alessandro de Medici."

(Enter MARIE.*)*

CATHERINE: Mother. What can this mean?

MARIE: What is it, my Catherine?

CATHERINE: A letter, addressed to me. Were my name not written here, I would think the messenger mistook me.

(Her mother takes it.)

MARIE: *(Reading it)* Is it news of Lorenzo? *(A beat)* Catherine, no. The Duke. How can he know you? Where can he have seen you?

CATHERINE: Lorenzo spoke of me, he says.

MARIE: No, this cannot be.

CATHERINE: A rendez-vous. What can he mean? I thought that Alessandro loved— That is, I heard it said that he and the countess— And now he wants to see me? But I am no one. The Countess is a woman of great beauty.

MARIE: It is Lorenzo who has done this. Your own brother would make you the Duke's mistress— or his whore!

CATHERINE: *(Imagining it)* But I am no one...

MARIE: I thought my son had reached the limit of his infamy. Yet this surpasses all. *(Crumples letter, drops it on the floor and exits)*

CATHERINE: Alessandro. It is frightening even to imagine. *(Retrieves the letter and unfolds it)* The Duke of Florence. By his own hand, this letter to me.

(Lights fade.)

3.3

(The rooms of the COUNTESS. *The* DUKE *and the* COUNTESS
in an embrace. She slips out of it and moves away from him.)

COUNTESS: You haven't answered me.

DUKE: What would you have me say?

COUNTESS: Say what is in your heart.

DUKE: That you have a most magnificent pair of legs.

COUNTESS: Have you heard nothing of what I said
tonight?

DUKE: Words, upon words. Do you think I came here to
talk?

COUNTESS: Words too are a form of love.

DUKE: You're dreaming, Ricarda.

COUNTESS: Yes, I dream—of a cause so great I would
sacrifice my honor, perhaps even my own child. But
what do kings know of a woman's dreams? Yours turn
to reality, by royal decree.

DUKE: Or my nightmares turn to bronze—the statues of
assassins that the people will call heroes.

COUNTESS: It need not be so. Think what power lives
in the name Alessandro. The power to turn "I wish"
to "I have." Hands join in fearful prayer, men hold their
breath at the sound.

DUKE: Must we talk of this?

COUNTESS: What is it to be a king? To be the difference
itself between good and evil. To have a hundred
thousand willing hands at the end of each royal arm.
To be the ray of sun that dries a woman's tears. To see

a father in the crowd hold up his son and say with
pride, Behold your king!

DUKE: Ricarda, please.

COUNTESS: How he would tremble, that weak old man
in the Vatican, if only you would spread your wings,
my eagle. The Emperor is so far. Your soldiers, so
devoted.

DUKE: Enough of this.

COUNTESS: Here is my dream, Alessandro: Florence,
free at last. Her honor and independence restored.
You have only to dream it too, to draw your sword
and say a single word, and you will wake to find
yourself a true king and a great one.

DUKE: If only such a transformation were so simple.

COUNTESS: Use your power to make it so. Proclaim the
city free. The people will venerate you, the father of
their freedom.

DUKE: The people despise me.

COUNTESS: Turn their hatred to love.

DUKE: You have greater faith in me than I have in
myself.

COUNTESS: There is goodness in you. I see it.

DUKE: You exaggerate me, madam.

COUNTESS: You are not evil within. I swear before God
you are not.

(He turns away.)

COUNTESS: There is yet time, Alessandro. Think how
young you are. Nothing in your life has been decided.
In the people's hearts there is a vast forgiveness for the
mistakes of their rulers. Say that you were ill advised,

your counselors misled you—that the fault lay with the
Cardinal.

DUKE: Cibo?

COUNTESS: He is a born intriguer. The people have no
love for him.

DUKE: You tempt me...

COUNTESS: It is within your reach. Take it. Save the city
and yourself.

DUKE: Can I be saved?

COUNTESS: Seize your place in history. Alessandro!

(They embrace. A moment, and he pulls away.)

DUKE: What a demon temptress you are, Ricarda...
Revolt against the Emperor and the Pope? Strike
against the source of my rule and power?

COUNTESS: Take that power for your own. It will be
your glory.

DUKE: It will be my death. Say what you will of me.
I may never live to see old age, nor deserve to, but I
do not leap headlong into my own grave.

COUNTESS: You are afraid.

DUKE: All Europe fears Charles V.

COUNTESS: Fear no less your people. Ignore them now
and see whether a corselet of body armor is enough to
save the Duke of Florence.

DUKE: Even that object I now lack.

COUNTESS: Let me help you find the courage to do this.

DUKE: *(Moving away from her)* Peace, woman! Enough of
politics from you.

COUNTESS: *(Pursuing him)* Then talk to me of love. You
pledged your heart a dozen times. I gave to you my

honor. Don't let my name be inscribed in infamy as your whore. Act from the heart, Alessandro, for your lover—if only this once and never again, but act now!

DUKE: *(He hesitates an instant, then breaks away.)* I must go. *(He begins dressing to leave.)*

COUNTESS: Is that your answer to me?

DUKE: I did not come here to be fatigued with grave matters of state.

COUNTESS: I bore you, then.

DUKE: You have said it, madam. I do not deny it. *(More tenderly)* Why do you interfere in these affairs, Ricarda? I come here to honor your beauty. I am not in need of yet another counselor. I am given a role, that of king. I do not play it to the people's taste, nor even to my own. *(A beat)* I come again another night, and you will play your role more expertly—that of a true woman. And mistress to the Duke of Florence.

COUNTESS: *Adieu*, Alessandro.

(She kisses him.)

(Enter CARDINAL. COUNTESS, *surprised breaks away and puts on a robe.)*

CARDINAL: Ah. Forgive me, Your Highness. I thought my sister-in-law was alone. How stupid of me.

DUKE: I can scarcely turn round of late without seeing your face, Cibo. Why is that?

CARDINAL: I am your counselor, Highness, and devoted servant.

DUKE: More distance to your devotion. The sight of priests disturbs my sleep. *(He exits.)*

CARDINAL: *(Bowing)* Highness. *(A beat)* Ricarda.

COUNTESS: Leave me!

CARDINAL: A word with you.

COUNTESS: Leave me.

(A beat)

CARDINAL: Until the morrow, then.

(He exits. She is alone. A beat)

COUNTESS: I thought to offer you a gift, my husband.
The return of your city. The resurrection of our
freedom. But instead I have squandered the treasure
of your honor. Now ridicule and doubt will stain the
final years of your noble life. Never again will you
lay your head upon my breast and hear the beating
of a heart worthy of you. I am sorry for it. Beyond
expression, I am sorry.

(Lights fade.)

3.4

*(A cellar room. PIERO, cloaked and hooded. The scene is in
near-darkness. Around him are four figures, also cloaked and
hooded.)*

PIERO: Patriots. Honest citizens of a dishonored city.
I summon you to this secret place tonight a fugitive,
charged with murder for defending my family's honor.
Each of you has a like grievance. Your sons are killed or
banished, your daughters disgraced, your homes and
fortunes stolen from you. Will the Medici cut down all
the noble families, rip from the soil our ancient roots,
as old as the city itself? Will they spill our blood and
we not spill theirs? My lords, now is the time for
vengeance. Where law is laid to ruin, let arms repair
the damage and restore us our honor. I declare myself
in rebellion against the bastard Duke. I form an army.
Take up arms and join me. One barrel of gunpowder in

the cellars of the citadel, and the German soldiers will be routed, Alessandro, powerless.

CONSPRIATOR 1: Who will lead this army?

PIERO: I shall lead it.

CONSPRIATOR 2: You, who are still a child?

CONSPRIATOR 1: Where is Philip your father?

CONSPRIATOR 3: If Piero will be the arm, then Philip must be the head of this endeavor, or how may we swear allegiance to it?

CONSPRIATOR 2: Someone comes!

(Enter PHILIP. CONSPIRATORS *cover themselves.)*

PHILIP: Do you conspire without me? You, my friends and fellow citizens? My son? Witness how you are shamed into meeting in darkness and disguise, as if criminals.

PIERO: It is Alessandro who turns honest men to criminals.

PHILIP: If we equal Alessandro in lawlessness, we surrender him our one advantage and most potent weapon.

PIERO: Father, we have surrendered our freedom. What advantage can remain?

PHILIP: Florence must win back her freedom, yes, but with law, not blood.

CONSPRIATOR 1: If you come to plead for law, Philip Strozzi, who will plead for my dead sons?

CONSPRIATOR 2: Or mine?

PIERO: The ruler of our city scorns the law, father.

PHILIP: Then we must appeal to Rome. Or to Spain and Charles himself.

CONSPRIATOR 2: You would turn to popes and emperors for justice?

CONSPRIATOR 1: Piero would raise an army. Will you lend your name to the effort?

PIERO: Join us, father. All the city will follow.

PHILIP: For sixty years I have lived a life of peace. Will you have me deny my own history?

PIERO: My father has chosen. Never let it be said that his son was more in love with words than with freedom.

PHILIP: To dishonor me, Piero, is to dishonor yourself.

PIERO: The time for speeches is past. *(He takes a cup and fills it with wine.)* Citizens. I drink to the death of the Medici.

PHILIP: *(Takes the cup and slams it down)* I will not drink to death. Nor will my child.

PIERO: *(Fills several cups with wine)* Will no one join me?

(Pause. One CONSPIRATOR steps forward and uncloaks.)

LOUISA: *(Stepping forward)* I join you, Piero.

PHILIP: Louisa, no.

(She takes a cup and drinks.)

PIERO: Will a woman outplay us in courage, lords?

PHILIP: In rashness, you are all outplayed by children.

PIERO: Join together, sound the alarm, and the banished citizens will rush to the gates of the city. We draw our swords and strike for justice!

(CONSPIRATORS pick up cups.)

ALL: Justice!

(LOUISA drops her cup)

LOUiSA: Father.

PHILIP: Louisa?

LOUiSA: Father, I am poisoned.

(She falls; PHILIP *and several others rush to her.)*

PHILIP: My daughter!

CONSPRIATOR 1: Call for a physician!

PHILIP: Help her, someone!

CONSPRIATOR 2: Open a window! Give her air!

PIERO: She has only fainted. She drank too quickly.

CONSPRIATOR 3: *(Feeling the pulse in her neck; amazed)*
She is dead.

PHILIP: My Louisa...

CONSPRIATOR 1: This is the work of the Duke!

CONSPRIATOR 2: His spies are among us.

CONSPRIATOR 1: Someone poisoned the wine.

CONSPRIATOR 2: Flee this place, citizens, before his
soldiers come for us!

(They exit. PHILIP *and* PIERO *remain with* LOUISA's *body.
A last conspirator stays behind: it is* TEBALDEO, *the painter.)*

PIERO: Will you talk now of justice, father? Will all the
words in all your precious books restore Louisa to us?
(He exits.)

TEBALDEO: Good sir, let me help you.

PHILIP: She but sleeps. A child's sweet blush, upon her
cheek. See it, there.

TEBALDEO: I shall always see it.

*(*TEBALDEO *picks up* LOUISA.)*

(They exit.)

4.1

(The DUKE's *palace)*

DUKE: Politics, cousin. It is ever a nasty and dispiriting craft, one that the ancient gods must have sent down as a plague upon man. To our discredit, we have perfected it.

LORENZO: Politics, you call it?

DUKE: Nothing more. To one who would say death to a king, death is the one reply. To pretend at rebellion is a fatal game. The Strozzis played and lost.

LORENZO: She was so young. It was a most cruel blow.

DUKE: Against a most cruel threat. I regret the wastefulness of it.

LORENZO: Do you?

DUKE: I have it on good authority that the assassin was Salviati's widow.

LORENZO: Unless it were someone higher.

DUKE: They say old Strozzi is fled to Venice.

LORENZO: His tears will overflow the canals. He loved his daughter most excessively.

DUKE: But exposed her life most rashly. Lay the blame at Philip's feet.

LORENZO: *(Letting some anger show)* His daughter is murdered and the fault lies with Philip?

DUKE: Are you so troubled by the death of my enemy?

LORENZO: I avow that death is sometimes a necessity, though regretted, as you say, for its waste. Highness. We have a matter to conclude, you and I.

DUKE: What matter?

LORENZO: My sister.

DUKE: Is it arranged?

LORENZO: Beyond even what you had hoped, my liege. Her eyes have known no repose since the promise of your love appeared so blindingly to her.

DUKE: Do you mock me, Lorenzo?

LORENZO: Never, my king. She adores you. Take pity on her, I beseech you, and grant her a royal audience.

DUKE: How may this be arranged?

LORENZO: It is done. My bedchamber, lord, at midnight. I will conduct you to the darkened room. You will disrobe and lie in wait for your bride of a night. At the stroke of twelve she will come to you, and beg you to be her ruler, in love as in law.

DUKE: My clever Lorenzaccio. What genius in your courtly scheming.

LORENZO: This meeting was fated to be, my lord. I am but an instrument of heaven.

DUKE: Heavenly instrument. You will be rewarded.

LORENZO: Your love is reward enough. But tell me, lord: your armor corselet?

DUKE: Still lost. There was none its equal in Italy. I suspect that painter of yours.

LORENZO: The artist is ever suspect, my lord.

DUKE: And with reason. But sweet cousin, I am excited strangely by this arrangement. I, in your own bed, with your own sibling flesh. She resembles you in fairness,

I think, and size. I shall transfer to her a portion of that affection I feel for you.

LORENZO: I must go, my lord.

DUKE: You look troubled, Lorenzo.

LORENZO: My heart was never lighter.

DUKE: Nor mine.

(*Exit separately*)

4.2

(*The* COUNTESS *at her home, with the* CARDINAL)

COUNTESS: Why do you pursue me? Am I your prey, and you the Pope's hound?

CARDINAL: You have acted on my advice, but acted alone.

COUNTESS: I know not what you mean.

CARDINAL: You are Alessandro's mistress. I have seen you in his embrace.

COUNTESS: And if I am?

CARDINAL: I hold your secret, and your fate, in my hands.

COUNTESS: Do with both what you will.

CARDINAL: I read indifference in your voice, but not your eye. You argued with him.

COUNTESS: Did you listen at the door like some gossiping chambermaid?

CARDINAL: You are unschooled in the ways of the court. Do you not know that a king's mistress must never speak of politics?

COUNTESS: Will the Cardinal instruct me in how a mistress must speak?

CARDINAL: Be more skillful in love and politics, and you will not be mistress, but queen.

COUNTESS: My ambition was for my city, not myself.

CARDINAL: Were those the city's lips on his? The city's legs he opened?

COUNTESS: How dare you.

(She tries to slap him, but he catches her arm and holds it.)

CARDINAL: Which was foremost in your heart, the people's fate or the countess's pleasure? *(He releases her.)*

COUNTESS: *(A beat. Turning away from him)* I know not.

CARDINAL: Ricarda. Reconcile yourself with Alessandro. Go to him now, assure him of your love and submission. Win his heart and you shall have in your hands the weapon to free your city. I shall show you how. A year from now, you will kneel at my feet and thank me.

COUNTESS: You, the true ruler of the city, in all but title.

(Sound of horses, off.)

CARDINAL: Return to Alessandro and do as I advise you.

COUNTESS: I will not.

CARDINAL: Did you not hear the sound of horses in the courtyard? Your husband returns to news of your betrayal, if you defy me now. *(He seizes her.)* Bow to me and I protect you against all. Say no to me again and I swear to you, you are lost.

(Enter the COUNT.*)*

COUNT: What scene is this?

(She moves away from the CARDINAL.*)*

COUNT: Enlighten me, I pray you.

CARDINAL: Countess, have I news for your husband?

COUNTESS: No!

(A beat. She turns to face the COUNT.*)*

I shall give the news, as I am its author.

CARDINAL: Ricarda, I forbid you—

COUNTESS: Come with me, Marcelo, that I may tell you a tale of betrayal—

CARDINAL: Ricarda!

COUNTESS: —though I would sacrifice my life to spare you the hearing of it.

(The COUNTESS *takes the* COUNT*'s hand and leads him swiftly from the room.)*

CARDINAL: How right it is and just—that in His wisdom, God created for women a special place in the most fiery region of hell. *(He exits.)*

4.3

(A deserted street in Florence. LORENZO, *alone. He is agitated; he paces, talking to himself.)*

LORENZO: He arrives. I show him in. 'Enter, my lord. Warm yourself.' He removes his sword, places it here. Or no, there, by the bed. "Will you remove your clothes, your highness?" No, I must not say it. No. "Lie here, my lord, in the bed. She comes to you." He does so. I remove the light. "Out of modesty, sire. My sister is virtuous and needs the courage that darkness brings." ...Or no. I leave the light. I want him to see it all, his own death. His trusted assassin, dagger in hand, lunging for his heart... Oh God, I am cold. I need to drink. I would empty a flagon in some

alehouse... But no. I mustn't drink, no. What is the
hour? There is time still, too much time. Moon, will you
not rise? Show your ghostly face, gaze down tonight
upon the murder of a tyrant... Oh words, words, eternal
talk! If there is someone in heaven, how he must laugh
at us all! What a grand comedy it is, these killers of
corpses here below, armless soldiers into the fray,
oh comic heroes, all! ...I have the devil's urge to dance.
If I let myself go, I would leap upon the heads of saints
and angels, from statue to statue like a flea, for I am like
a flea and Alessandro, a lion... I will not do it with his
back turned, though he may overpower me... The city
will rise up. The streets, alive again with freedom.
Glory and triumph and tears, I am raised upon their
shoulders— No. Beware pride, the demon's vision,
as Philip warned me... Did I hear the hour sound? No,
no, it was the half-hour... This is how the virgin bride
must feel before the moment of her consummation.
My marriage bed this bed shall be. I am wedded tonight
to my fate. I give myself to it, with blood and cries of
joy and all.

(Enter CATHERINE.*)*

CATHERINE: Lorenzo.

LORENZO: Catherine?

CATHERINE: I was on my way to see you.

LORENZO: I should not be seen, save by the one I have
chosen. Why have you come?

CATHERINE: I seek an answer from you. Why did
Alessandro write to me, Lorenzo?

LORENZO: Did he?

CATHERINE: A letter, begging to see me. He professed
love for me.

LORENZO: *(Ushering her out)* Catherine, return home to mother.

CATHERINE: *(Refusing to leave)* You spoke to him of me. What did you say?

LORENZO: That you are virtuous and he without hope.

(He tries to escort her out again. She breaks away.)

CATHERINE: How do you know that to be true?

LORENZO: Catherine.

CATHERINE: The Duke of Florence declares his desire for me. I, who am no one, caretaker to an aged woman, pledged to a convent and a life of silence. But what will I dream of those long nights of winter, I who have hardly lived a life at all? A king writes to me. A king, Lorenzo! Might I not at least see him and know his intentions?

LORENZO: Will the lamb sit down with the wolf and talk of intentions?

CATHERINE: Love, they say, can transform nature.

LORENZO: Oh, love!

CATHERINE: I cannot believe the ruler of our city is so much the beast as you and mother say. But even were he, would not a kind heart work some healing change upon him?

LORENZO: You would heal the Duke of Florence?

CATHERINE: If it be within my abilities.

LORENZO: Oh laugh at us, heaven! Let the sky crack with your laughter! The sister would heal a king while the brother would kill one. Oh, it is beyond comic.

CATHERINE: What do these words mean, Lorenzo? Are you mad? Do you laugh at me?

LORENZO: I laugh, knowing that I am laughed at.
And yes, I am mad, I must be. Go home, Catherine,
I beg you, and if you will not be begged, then I order
you. There are movements this night of earth and sky
that will work more change upon us than ever you or
I can foresee.

CATHERINE: Lorenzo, my brother—

LORENZO: Go home. Await news of me. Remember,
despite what men will say, I have acted for you,
and for mother, and for freedom.

(Exit LORENZO. CATHERINE *watches him go, then exits.)*

4.4

*(*DUKE *at court, attended by* NICOLINI, RUCCELLI, *a*
SERVANT, *and* VENTURI, *the silk merchant. The* DUKE
is drinking. All are laughing. Enter the CARDINAL.*)*

DUKE: Drink with us, Cardinal, since you have come.
Or do you not drink?

CARDINAL: Only in service to God, sire. Never in
service to my king.

DUKE: It would be physic for you. Wine to heat the
blood. You have blood, Cibo?

CARDINAL: As God has created me, sire, yes.

(Enter VALORI.*)*

DUKE: I thought it was Charles and his lapdog the Pope
created you. I don't know that we can blame God.

CARDINAL: *(Confidentially)* A word with you, your
highness.

DUKE: I am plagued with words.

CARDINAL: Sire—

DUKE: Is silence a quality unheard of at court? Whisper your plots in some more willing ear.

CARDINAL: Though I risk your displeasure, sire, I have news that I must convey, or I risk much more. Lorenzo has reserved two horses this night and given orders they be held for him at the bridge.

DUKE: This cannot be so.

CARDINAL: I have it on good authority, sire.

DUKE: I have it on better authority—my own. Lorenzo is engaged in a royal matter this night.

CARDINAL: It is my duty to alert you, sire. He was seen not an hour ago in the public square, talking madly to himself.

DUKE: Lorenzo, being Lorenzo.

CARDINAL: He was overheard declaring that a king would die tonight.

DUKE: Oh, I die tonight, Cibo, yes—the dying that follows pleasure. But what do priests know of earthly ecstasy? No, don't answer me that.

CARDINAL: Be forewarned, I beg you.

DUKE: Be less deceived, I charge you. You all despise my Lorenzaccio. But I tell you this: I would trade the lot of you for Lorenzo de Medici, noon or night.

(*Enter* LORENZO.)

LORENZO: My lord. Are you ready?

DUKE: Is it the hour, cousin?

LORENZO: Near midnight.

DUKE: A timely rescue. I can scarcely breathe in these rooms. The air is thick with counsel.

LORENZO: We must hurry, sire. Your prize is perhaps already in place.

DUKE: What gloves do I wear? Those for war? Or for love?

LORENZO: For love, my lord.

(*Exit* DUKE *and* LORENZO.)

VALORI: What do you make of this, your eminence?

CARDINAL: That God chooses the instrument of His divine will, whether man consent or not.

(*Lights*)

4.5

(LORENZO's *room. The* DUKE *is nearly drunk.*)

LORENZO: Enter, my lord. Warm yourself.

DUKE: Yes, I am strangely chilled... Where is she?

LORENZO: In the next room.

DUKE: Lorenzo.

LORENZO: Sire?

DUKE: Will she talk a great deal? I cannot abide talkative women.

LORENZO: She will utter not a word.

DUKE: I have a strange sensation—that if it were you who came to me now, in this bed, and not she— how we might...laugh and talk. Careless together, as two schoolboys.

LORENZO: Yes. (*A beat*) Let me take your sword, sire.

DUKE: No. I keep a blade near to hand, always.

(LORENZO *moves to take the lamp.*)

DUKE: Do you take the light?

LORENZO: My sister...she is virtuous and needs the darkness.

DUKE: Your hands tremble.

(LORENZO starts to leave with the lamp.)

DUKE: Leave the light.

(He replaces it, starts again to leave.)

DUKE: Lorenzo.

(He halts)

DUKE: Why did you arrange for horses at the bridge tonight?

LORENZO: *(A beat; he is caught)* I thought to flee.

DUKE: Why?

LORENZO: Fear, my lord.

DUKE: While I live you need not fear any man. You are loved by Alessandro, Duke of Florence. I am your armor.

(Again, LORENZO starts to leave.)

DUKE: Will you stay?

LORENZO: Sire?

DUKE: Nearby me. While your sister and I...?

LORENZO: Very near, sire. Always.

DUKE: You might watch us. Even join us.

LORENZO: As you wish, my lord.

DUKE: An embrace, sweet cousin, before you bring her.

(They embrace and the DUKE kisses LORENZO. They break off, but remain close.)

DUKE: You are cold. Your face so pale. You worry me.

(LORENZO *exits.* DUKE, *uneasy, sits on the bed and begins to undress.*)

DUKE: I feel now strangely out of spirit for this thing...
If blessed sleep would come, and not this woman,
I might well prefer it... That comet sighted in the
Eastern sky. My counselors declare it a manifest of
nature's discontent. And were it but a comet, nothing
more? A piece of fiery heaven come loose, as a ceiling
tile in an aging palace falls. Yet men cry 'God's terrible
judgment' and seek to know the cause, as if knowing
were a benefit. Ignorance might be envied, if it breed
a dreamless sleep, as it does in children... (*He hears
something.*) She comes.

(*Enter* LORENZO, *in a woman's long cloak, hooded,
so he cannot be recognized.*)

DUKE: Approach me, Catherine. Give me your hands.

(*The* DUKE *begins to lead him to the bed.*)

DUKE: You tremble, as your brother did... You fear me.
Yet would I be loved more and feared less... I well love
your brother, as I think he does love me... Let me see
you... Reveal yourself, I say. Your king commands it.
Reveal.

(LORENZO *reveals himself.*)

DUKE: Lorenzaccio. What play is this?

LORENZO: A tragedy, my lord, that ends in death.

(*He stabs the* DUKE.)

DUKE: No, my Lorenzo.

(*They struggle.* LORENZO *stabs the* DUKE *several times.*)

DUKE: Dear Lorenzo. No!

(LORENZO *slits the* DUKE's *throat. The* DUKE *collapses.*
LORENZO, *stunned, surveys the scene.*)

LORENZO: Here lies my answer. Not heaven called me, but a demon. For how can this be greatness?

(A knock on the door, off, startles him. Frightened)

SCORON: Master?

(Enter quickly his servant, SCORON.)

SCORON: Are you wounded?

(LORENZO shakes his head.)

SCORON: This was your enemy, then? Who was the villain? *(He turns the DUKE over.)* Christ Jesus, the Duke of Florence! Master. What have you done?

LORENZO: *(At the window)* Breathe the air of Florence, Scoron. Has it changed? Does it taste sweeter to you now?

SCORON: Master, we flee the city.

LORENZO: Is there a taste of freedom to it?

SCORON: Be not distracted, master, I beg you.

LORENZO: I thought, if Alessandro did not breathe it more, the very air might transform. But no. It is as it ever was.

SCORON: Now, master. Please. The horses wait at the bridge.

LORENZO: Sleep now, cousin. One man is free in Florence at last.

(They exit. Lights)

5.1

(The Ducal palace, the next morning. Sounds of a crowd offstage. Enter VENTURI, *who put his ear to a door, straining to hear a conversation on the other side.* VALORI *enters.)*

VENTURI: What news, Sir Envoy?

VALORI: None. Or rather, none that encourages.

VENTURI: Is the Duke returned?

VALORI: He is not.

VENTURI: Absent all the night.

VALORI: And these morning hours.

VENTURI: There is a crowd at the gates, my lord,
that feasts on rumor and grows larger by the minute.

VALORI: Can the soldiers not disperse them?

VENTURI: The Cardinal forbids it. He has ordered wine
be brought to them, and cakes.

VALORI: To purchase their passivity. This Cibo is ruling
all in the absence of Alessandro. He has locked himself
away in the Duke's apartments and called in his privy
councilors.

VENTURI: I overheard these councilors, sir, in whispered
conversation. They fear hangings.

VALORI: Hangings? Whose?

VENTURI: Their own, sir, and ours. If some tragedy
has befallen the Duke, there may be riots and reprisals.
The palace could be taken.

(Enter NICOLINI, *a counselor.)*

VALORI: Here is Lord Nicolini. Good sir, what news?

NICOLINI: I am not at liberty to spread news, sir.

VALORI: Weren't you in audience with the Cardinal?

NICOLINI: It is possible that I was, sir. But not certain.

VALORI: Is there news of the Duke?

NICOLINI: The Duke, sir, citing unconfirmed rumor, which I do not spread, may have...

VALORI: What, sir?

NICOLINI: May have vanished.

VALORI: How can this be?

NICOLINI: I do not say it can. Or even that it is.

VALORI: Messengers come and go from the palace. Do you know of these, Lord Nicolini?

NICOLINI: I am not at liberty to say, sir, if I know, and if, what. But I can suggest to you, unofficially, and, be it understood, anonymously, that messengers are sent to the Emperor's generals at Arezzo and Pisa.

VALORI: Dare Cibo go so far?

NICOLINI: Further, sir. A more urgent messenger is sent.

VALORI: To whom, sir?

VENTURI: To whom, yes.

NICOLINI: According to sources unnamed: to Cosimo.

VALORI: Cosimo?

VENTURI: Cosimo?

NICOLINI: Be astonished, sirs. Cosimo.

VENTURI: May I ask a question, my lord?

NICOLINI: I am not at liberty to answer questions.
Yet I cannot prevent a question from lodging, sir,
on its own initiative, within my ear.

VENTURI: Who is Cosimo?

NICOLINI: 'Who is Cosimo?' Do you jest?

(Enter another counselor, RUCCELLI.)

RUCCELLI: The crowd at the gates grows restless.

VALORI: Wine has been given them, Lord Ruccelli,
on the Cardinal's orders.

RUCCELLI: They demand answers with their wine.
The city is wild with rumor.

NICOLINI: Someone must make a statement to the
people.

RUCCELLI: Yes, but who, Nicolini?

VENTURI: *(A brilliant idea)* What about the Duke?

(They all stare at VENTURI.)

RUCCELLI: Who is this person?

VENTURI: Venturi, my lord, at your service. Holder of
the royal monopoly on silks.

(They move away from him and return to their conversation.)

VALORI: What do you know of this order for arrest,
Ruccelli?

RUCCELLI: I am not at liberty to say what I know.
However. Anonymously. Lorenzo de Medici has
fled the city.

VALORI: Lorenzo?

RUCCELLI: I do not state it as fact.

VALORI: But Lorenzo was in the company of the Duke
last night.

NICOLINI: Do you state that as fact?

(Enter the CARDINAL.*)*

VALORI: Your eminence. Some news of the situation,
I beg you.

CARDINAL: *(To* NICOLINI *and* RUCCELLI*)* A delegation of
the citizens has entered the grand hall.

NICOLINI: Where are the German soldiers?

CARDINAL: Lord Ruccelli. Announce to the citizens that
the Duke cannot receive them.

RUCCELLI: But they will ask me why.

CARDINAL: The Duke is sleeping. He was at a masked
ball and returned late to the palace. Lord Nicolini.
Have the soldiers distribute more wine to the crowd.

NICOLINI: Very good, your eminence.

VALORI: Cardinal Cibo, I demand information.

CARDINAL: Alessandro de Medici is dead.

VALORI: Dead!

VENTURI: Dead, you say?

CARDINAL: Murdered.

VENTURI: What?

VALORI: It is beyond belief!

VENTURI: Who is the murderer?

CARDINAL: Lorenzo de Medici, as I forewarned.

VALORI: This is astonishing.

VENTURI: The people will be in rebellion.

CARDINAL: The people will know nothing until I
consent that they know. And any one of you who
feeds them the rumor of Alessandro's death will face
his own death in turn.

VALORI: But the Emperor must be notified. And the Pope.

CARDINAL: A royal messenger has been dispatched to each. Order will be maintained until a successor is in place.

VALORI: But Cibo. This is a dangerous strategy. When will you tell the populace?

CARDINAL: When the German garrison has been reinforced. *(He exits.)*

RUCCELLI: It is my observation that a successor is already in place. But I do not confirm that I said so.

VENTURI: Lord Nicolini. This Cosimo. Who is he?

NICOLINI: Cosimo de Medici. Blood relative to the late Duke. It will be made to appear a lawful succession.

VENTURI: Cosimo is to be the next Duke?

RUCCELLI: We do not know, think or state it. But unofficially: count upon it, sirs.

VALORI: What kind of man is he?

VENTURI: Yes, what kind?

VALORI: What is his relation to the Vatican?

VENTURI: What is his position on silks?

RUCCELLI: A boy of seventeen. Dull-witted.

NICOLINI: Malleable.

RUCCELLI: Possibly suffering from a serious imbalance of the humours.

NICOLINI: An excess of phlegm.

RUCCELLI: If not yellow bile.

NICOLINI: Sickly. Inexperienced.

RUCCELLI: Unambitious. The perfect lump of clay in Cibo's hands.

NICOLINI: Although...

RUCCELLI: Although... We deny having said so. Address yourselves to Cibo, gentlemen. The Cardinal rules the city.

(*Exit* RUCCELLI *and* NICOLINI.)

VALORI: This is most disturbing, Venturi.

VENTURI: Indeed, my lord. The Cardinal purchases his silk directly from Rome.

VALORI: I take my leave, sir.

(*Exit* VALORI; VENTURI, *his back to him, fails to notice his exit.*)

VENTURI: (*Ruminating*) And yet, when one thinks upon it. A funeral. All pennants and bunting in the black of mourning. The entire city, displaying its sorrow, everywhere. In silk. And the new Duke, this Cosimo. He will want his own colors. Make his own mark, so to speak. Yes. (*To* VALORI) Oh, *most* disturbing, my lord, most— Lord Valori? (*He exits, anxiously.*)

5.2

(*Venice. The rooms of* PHILIP. *Enter* PHILIP *and* LORENZO.)

PHILIP: My circumstances are much reduced here in Venice. Still, there is a bed for you, and food.

(PHILIP *brings* LORENZO *food and drink.*)

LORENZO: You have aged ten years in the days since you left Florence.

PHILIP: I have buried a daughter. It is an unnatural act for the father to bury the child. And worse, I fear I may repeat it.

LORENZO: You speak of Piero?

PHILIP: He is with me here in Venice. He tries to raise an army, if such a band of drunkards may be called army. They long to put Florence to the torch and hang Alessandro at the gates of the citadel.

LORENZO: An impossible task, my lord.

(*Enter* PIERO.)

PIERO: Impossible for traitors and cowards like you.

PHILIP: Piero, I caution you.

PIERO: Florence needs not caution but blood, that of Alessandro and those who took his money and kissed his cheek, who helped him rape the city that once was ours.

LORENZO: And will be ours again.

PIERO: You will curse that day, Lorenzo de Medici, for it will be the day you hang.

PHILIP: I will not have these hateful words.

PIERO: Words are your currency, father. It is deeds you scorn.

PHILIP: The deeds you propose are bloodshed and suicide.

PIERO: Unless you join with us. The people will not rise from their table for a Piero. Oh, but for a Philip what will they not do. Horses and arms and all.

LORENZO: And all, unnecessary. Will you hear me, Philip?

PIERO: What news can traitors offer patriots but lies and betrayal?

(LORENZO *places a key before* PHILIP.)

PHILIP: A key?

LORENZO: To my rooms in Florence. Were you to unlock that door, a terrifying sight would greet you. A dead king.

PIERO: What do you say?

LORENZO: Alessandro de Medici, the late Duke of Florence.

PHILIP: Lorenzo.

LORENZO: Slain by this hand.

PIERO: It cannot be so.

PHILIP: Have you truly done it, Lorenzo? Have you made yourself our Brutus?

LORENZO: I have murdered my cousin, who loved me. His blood soaked the bed I dreamed in.

PIERO: What proof? This is nothing more than lies.

LORENZO: I tore open his flesh and watched the life pour from him in such scarlet waves as I thought would drown me. I see now that I am as Alessandro was.

PHILIP: The people will see you as you wished. Lorenzo de Medici, the liberator of Florence.

PIERO: These words are daggers that murder my hope. A curse on you if you have stolen my revenge from me. I ride to our army and to Florence. If any man has right to seize this fallen crown, it is I. (*He exits.*)

PHILIP: My son will not hear me. The clamor of his ambition overwhelms all my words.

LORENZO: None of Piero's blood need be spilled, Philip. At this moment, citizens take sword in hand and surround the citadel. The banished return in triumph to their homes. Do you not see it?

PHILIP: Our freedom restored to us.

LORENZO: A single spark, they say, can set a forest aflame. The flash of one sword can light all a century. History itself confirms it.

PHILIP: A crier approaches, with news.

(PHILIP *moves to open the window. Indistinctly, the sounds of a crier from the streets below.*)

LORENZO: He will announce the end of tyranny in Florence, the triumph of the people. The finest republic ever seen in Europe, ours for the taking. Philip! I taste freedom in the air at last.

(PHILIP *closes the window.*)

LORENZO: What is it?

(PHILIP *doesn't respond.* LORENZO *moves and opens the window. When he does, we hear the crier distinctly.*)

PHILIP: Close the window.

LORENZO: No.

PHILIP: Close it, Lorenzo, I beg you.

CRIER: Citizens of Venice! Four thousand gold florins to the man, noble or commoner, who will kill Lorenzo de Medici, assassin and traitor to his country. By order of Cosimo de Medici, the new Duke of Florence.

(*A beat; they both hear something.*)

PHILIP: Someone mounts the stair.

(*A knock at the door, off.*)

PHILIP: Hide yourself in here. Quickly. Go!

(*Exeunt.*)

5.3

(PAOLO *and* SOFIA, *the two cloth sellers, set up their stand on the street in Florence.*)

PAOLO: This is too far away.

SOFIA: It's just right.

PAOLO: It's too far. We can't see the speakers from here.

SOFIA: We can hear them, that's bad enough.

PAOLO: The location is all wrong.

SOFIA: It's perfect. People go by in a good mood, they buy because they're hopeful. They come back in a bad mood, they buy because they're depressed.

PAOLO: I want to see him with my own two eyes. Cosimo, the glorious new ruler of my city.

SOFIA: Paolo, don't start.

PAOLO: The new abomination sent down upon our heads without our consent.

SOFIA: Maybe with this new one, things will improve.

PAOLO: We trade a lecherous butcher for a half-wit puppet, that's improvement? (*His set piece*) It wasn't always like this. Years ago, this city was like that palace there.

SOFIA: Oh no. Please.

(*A man enters. He wears a hooded cloak; his face is concealed by shadow.*)

SOFIA: Paolo, a customer. (*Aside, to heaven*) Thank you, God!

PAOLO: Good morning, sir. May I show you something in a hopeful color? Here for the coronation, are you, sir?

HOODED MAN: For a funeral.

PAOLO: No funerals in Florence, sir. Only yards of bunting waving from every damn window of the citadel. That idiot Venturi must have made a fortune. But you refer to the late Duke, sir, if I divine your meaning. Tragic ending, eh?

HOODED MAN: The tragedy is for freedom.

PAOLO: Ah, you are a patriot. *(Confidentially)* Be it known: this stand is operated by true Florentine patriots. In fact, we have a special this morning for patriots only, ten percent off every item we carry.

HOODED MAN: *(Angrily)* Do you sell cloths? Why do you not take up a sword to slice the throats of German soldiers?

PAOLO: I, sir?

HOODED MAN: Alessandro bled the city of courage. Now only slaves are left.

SOFIA: Lord Lorenzo was no slave, sir.

HOODED MAN: A curse on Lorenzo de Medici!

SOFIA: Fie, sir!

PAOLO: To the patriots of Florence, he is a hero.

HOODED MAN: He is a murderer.

SOFIA: Not so, not so!

PAOLO: Did you even know him, sir, as we do?

SOFIA: He shopped at this very stand.

PAOLO: We were intimate, sir. He often sought my advice, being very young in years and over fond of women and drink and other dissipations of the body.

(LORENZO uncovers; SOFIA sees him, PAOLO does not.)

PAOLO: He saw me as a wise and beneficent elder brother—

SOFIA: Paolo.

PAOLO: 'Gratias ago,' he would say to me in passable Latin, 'I thank you, good Paolo,' and I would place my arm upon his shoulders, thus—

SOFIA: Pssst!

PAOLO: *(Seeing him)* Lord Lorenzo.

LORENZO: What advice for me now?

SOFIA: Cover, my lord! Cover!

PAOLO: There is a price upon your head!

LORENZO: Too rich a price, too poor a head. I have had enough of disguise. I go forth now as myself, Lorenzo de Medici, assassin and traitor.

SOFIA: No, you must flee, my lord!

LORENZO: Where? In all of Europe I am hunted. On the very street corners of heaven, God himself has hung the Cardinal's warrant for my execution.

PAOLO: But it is madness to come here.

LORENZO: Madness is to make death the purpose of your life, all to no purpose. To have faith in men, who cry for freedom, but when the moment comes to purchase it, they argue the price, until the moment and freedom are gone... I sought to be what I am not, to change what cannot change. That too is madness.

PAOLO: Let us hide you, my lord, till nightfall.

SOFIA: Then you might slip away by dark.

LORENZO: I am come now for my reward, good citizens. I may not leave without it.

(PAOLO *and* SOFIA, *sensing danger, slip away and exit.*
Sounds of a crowd. Fanfare. LORENZO *turns away, toward*
the square where the ceremony will take place. A man,
cloaked and hooded, appears behind him.

(*The* CARDINAL *appears upon a dais, leading the city's new*
ruler, COSIMO DE MEDICI, *before the crowd.* COSIMO *is*
young, barely more than a boy. LORENZO *stands and*
watches as the CARDINAL *speaks.*)

CARDINAL: Citizens of Florence. By the power vested
in me by the Emperor Charles, and by His Holiness the
Pope, I do present you now the ruler of this your city...
Cosimo de Medici, Duke of Florence!

(*As* COSIMO *is led forward the man slowly approaches*
LORENZO. LORENZO *sees him but does not attempt to flee;*
he is not even surprised at the man's approach. During the
speech, the man will stab LORENZO *to death.*)

(COSIMO *delivers the speech with difficulty.* CARDINAL
stands at his shoulder and prompts or corrects him as needed.)

COSIMO: Good citizens. Know you this: I, Cosimo, make
these solemn oaths. First, to rule with justice—as much
justice as it shall take to rule firmly. Second, to avenge
the cruel murder of my noble cousin, Alessandro de
Medici. Let death be the answer to his death. Let statues
be erected in his honor. These things be done, in the
name of this great city. God bless Florence!

(*The* CARDINAL *and* COSIMO *join hands and raise their*
arms in triumph.)

COSIMO & CARDINAL. God bless Florence!

(*Trumpets sound. Opposite, the body of* LORENZO, *watched*
over by his assassin. He uncovers his head and we see that the
murderer is PIERO.)

END OF PLAY

www.ingramcontent.com/pod-product-compliance
Lightning Source LLC
Chambersburg PA
CBHW070017110426
42741CB00034B/2076